THE MISSING CONNECTION BETWEEN BUSINESS AND THE UNIVERSITIES

THE MISSING CONNECTION BETWEEN BUSINESS AND THE UNIVERSITIES

Ernest A. Lynton

John W. McCormack Institute of Public Affairs
University of Massachusetts at Boston

American
Council on
Education

Macmillan
Publishing
Company

NEW YORK

Collier Macmillan Publishers
LONDON

The American Council on Education/Macmillan Series on Higher Education

Macmillan Publishing Company
866 Third Avenue, New York, N. Y. 10022

Collier Macmillan Canada, Inc.

Library of Congress Catalog Card Number: 84–2849

Printed in the United States of America

printing number
1 2 3 4 5 6 7 8 9 10

Library of Congress Cataloging in Publication Data

Lynton, E. A. (Ernest A.)
  The missing connection between business and the
universities.

  (The American Council on Education/Macmillan series
in higher education)
  Bibliography: p.
  Includes index.
  1. Industry and education—United States. 2. Occupa-
tional training—United States. I. Title. II. Series.
LC1085.L96 1984   378'.103   84–2849
ISBN 0-02-919280-3

FOR CARLA, DAVID AND ERIC

Contents

Foreword

AMERICA NEEDS a new order of occupational education and training to cope with the dramatic changes in technology and rationalization of the economy. The automatic growth of the economy and its attendant standard of living of the past several decades are no longer assured, and the American way of economic life is in peril. The best defense we have for keeping any semblance of economic well-being is to have the most competent, highest-quality work force possible.

The two American institutions that have contributed most toward our nation's growth—the university and the corporation—must find new methods of collaboration to build the human capital needed to cope with this onrush of change and challenge. Dr. Ernest A. Lynton's book goes a long way toward outlining the issues, reviewing the problems, and describing examples of employer-provided education and training. It also delves into the sensitive issues and attitudes of education-work relations, which can represent substantial barriers to educator-employer collaboration.

It is plain from Dr. Lynton's book that we cannot tolerate competition between educators and employers over continuing education "turf." There is more than enough challenge and work for both sectors, as well as a rational breakdown of responsibility. In principle, simple logic indicates that educators should handle generic education and employers specific job training. Of course, this simplicity is compounded by the many variables relating to separate disciplines or fields, size and nature of the organization, rate of change, and other factors.

Another force that naturally drives the division of effort is the fact that educators, by and large, foster as much education as possible while employers try to keep the amount of education to a minimum, since it represents costs that must be included in the price of their products or services.

Dr. Lynton makes a compelling case for a new *process* of educator-employer collaboration. Direct relationships between those who share ownership, accountability, and real knowledge of needs and resources will make the new educational relationship work. Although the government should have a role, mostly through providing incentives for and removing disincentives from educator-employer collaboration, it is the direct connections that will produce the needed work force.

Dr. Lynton, who has done much research in this area, clearly identifies the elements of the issue and outlines constructive approaches to building a national occupational education enterprise to meet the needs of the future. We highly recommend careful attention to this book.

ROBERT L. CRAIG
Vice President
American Society for Training and Development

Preface:
The Missing Connection

THIS BOOK ARISES from a profound concern about the limited role of colleges and universities in the substantial system of employee education and training. Even a cursory survey reveals a connection missing between this considerable array of instructional activities and the present system of higher education. In recent years, both private- and public-sector employers have multiplied their expenditures for what is now usually called "human resource development," or HRD. Employers spend tens of billions of dollars each year on organized instruction ranging from a few hours of training to prolonged and sophisticated courses, all intended to enhance the occupational effectiveness of the participants. A substantial portion of this activity is designed for college-trained employees in professional, supervisory, and managerial positions. Much of it is quite generic. Yet only a small fraction is directly provided by colleges and universities. Most of the instruction is either organized in-house by the employer, provided by a union or professional association, or supplied under contract by a growing number of third-party vendors. This last category of providers has in the aggregate grown so much that one commonly speaks of a training industry.

Higher education has good reason to be seriously concerned about its limited connection to human resource development. For one thing, it is obviously missing out on a substantial educational market. The declining number of college-age

young people constitutes a serious threat to the financial
stability of both public and private colleges and universities,
unless they manage to reach a wider clientele. This alone
should be adequate motivation for a more aggressive stance
with respect to employer-sponsored instruction.

Much more is at stake for higher education than access to a
potentially lucrative market. The missing connection with the
vast system of employee education both reflects and intensifies
the dangerous isolation of academic institutions from their external constituencies. This isolation is in part responsible for
widespread public disillusion with higher education. It has also
resulted in substantial shortcomings in the traditional preparatory function of colleges and universities. The absence of close
and continuing contact with the outside world leaves too much
of a gap between theory and practice. Degree programs both in
professional fields and in the arts and sciences often fail to
prepare students adequately for future effectiveness as workers
and as citizens. The chorus of criticism is growing.

Society, like nature, tends to fill a vacuum. If existing institutions do not meet an important societal need, other mechanisms are usually created to fill the gap. Clearly this has already
happened to a considerable extent in human resources development. Employers as well as professional and labor associations have developed their own alternatives to the existing institutions of higher education. Many nonacademic observers no
longer see much need for greater involvement by colleges and
universities; they view any attempts at increasing the connection as purely a matter of educational institutions fighting for
survival.

In one sense, this book reflects such self-interest. It is written by someone who has spent his entire professional career in
higher education and who wants to help colleges and universities in their fight for survival. Yet the book is also based on the
conviction that a greater role by these institutions in the development and maintenance of occupational effectiveness is much
more than a matter of academic self-interest. The current situation is not only dangerous for higher education, it is also less
than optimal for employers and employees. Lack of systematic

planning, fragmentation of offerings, and excessive emphasis on immediate utility tend to result in an approach which may not be cost effective and which does not produce optimal results. More cooperation between the worlds of work and of education, and the development of a real dialogue with a two-way flow of ideas and criticism between employers and educators, can lead to a better balance between breadth and specificity, between long-range considerations and immediate needs. Both sides are likely to gain. In addition, the resulting closer relationship between educators and employers, between learning and work, is likely to have substantial societal benefits. It will enhance the pertinence and the responsiveness of higher education, and it is likely to lead also to greater sensitivity by all concerned to the importance of finding the best way of developing and maintaining human resources.

However, this will not happen without substantial adaptations in the attitudes, policies, and procedures of our colleges and universities. It will require, as well, a broader conception of the importance of human resources on the part of employers and also of policymakers and legislators at all levels of government. The book addresses itself to these changes in the hope that all constituencies, not only higher education, may profit from its suggestions.

Acknowledgments

My INTEREST IN employer-sponsored education, which extends back several years, received early support from Rexford Moon. In 1978, when he was in charge of the College Board Project, "Future Directions for a Learning Society," I discussed with him my conviction that colleges and universities should make a greater effort to provide educational services to groups of employees through contracts with their employers or organizations. He commissioned a paper on that subject for his project, and this gave me my first opportunity to explore it systematically. Two years later I launched into the pertinent issues more intensively when Fred Crossland, then at the Ford Foundation, asked me to write a background paper for the foundation on the "shadow educational system," which was then just beginning to receive a good deal of attention. Later he was my program officer on a grant that allowed me to pursue the subject further. His continuing interest and support have meant a great deal to me.

Whatever I have learned about employer-sponsored education is largely due to the patience with which many experts in the fields received me and allowed me to ask questions for hours at a time. For their help I am extremely grateful to the following: John Budlong and Harry Evarts of American Management Associations; Robert Craig of the American Society for Training and Development; Donald Fronzaglia of Polaroid; Martin Feldman of the New York Fashion Institute of Technology; Bud Hodgkinson, formerly President of National Training Laboratories and now Senior Fellow at the Institute for Educational Leadership; John Jenness of Consolidated Edison;

Henry Kaufman of the Polytechnic Institute of New York;
Ronald Kropowski of Chase Manhattan; Norman Kurland of
the New York Board of Regents; the late Calvin Lee of Pruden-
tial; Seymour Lusterman and his colleagues Ruth Shaeffer and
Alan Janger of the Conference Board; William May, dean of
the NYU School of Business and former CEO of American
Can; Harper Moulton, Charles Brown, and Scott Moore of International Business Machines; Charles Sener of the Bell Systems Center in Lisle, Illinois; David Tyre of Exxon; and
Michael Walsh of Continental Grain.

In addition to giving me much of their time for extended
visits, some of these individuals also provided helpful comments on early papers and several participated in a day-long
meeting at the Ford Foundation that helped me a great deal in
clarifying my ideas. Much of the benefit I derived from that session was due to Mike Timpane, at the time just moving from
the National Institute of Education to Teachers College, who
moderated the meeting superbly. I am also grateful to Bob
Arns of the University of Vermont; James Baughman of General Electric; Dennis Doyle of the American Enterprise Institute; Alden Dunham and David Robinson of the Carnegie Corporation; Badi Foster, who was about to create the Aetna Institute for Corporate Education; E. T. Keough of Western Electric; Martin Meyerson, President Emeritus of Penn; Henry
Winkler, President of the University of Cincinnati; Roger Yarrington of the American Association of Community and Junior
Colleges; and Kenneth Young of the National University Continuing Education Association; all of whom contributed a great
deal to that very useful session. Others who helped me with
written comments included Frank Blount of American Telephone and Telegraph, Chester Francke of General Motors,
Martin Krasney, then of the ARCO Corporation, and Kevin
Reilly of the New York Board of Regents.

Twice I profited from opportunities to obtain information
and views on employer-sponsored education from a European
perspective. D. S. Markwell not only welcomed me to the
Unilever Training Centre for a lengthy visit but also invited
Roy Harrison from the National Coal Board and Roy Hamp-

ton from the Dunlop Corporation to join us for a discussion from which I learned much about conditions in the United Kingdom. On another occasion I benefited a great deal from a meeting in Paris with officials of IBM France.

There are a few people to whom I turned repeatedly for advice: Nevser Stacey at NIE and her former colleague Marc Tucker, David Riesman at Harvard, Bob Zemsky at Penn, Paul Barton and Gerry Gold of the National Institute for Work and Learning, Tony Carnevale of ASTD, Donald Schön at MIT and, time and again, Russ Edgerton from the American Association for Higher Education. I am particularly grateful for the help several of them gave me as I turned my focus from corporate education to a broader look at the condition of higher education in the United States. During the past year I became increasingly convinced that the limited role of colleges and universities in the delivery of employer-sponsored education is symptomatic of a broader failure of higher education to meet the changing needs of society. This book bridges and combines my earlier work with my current interest in the future of universities. Generous grants from the Carnegie Corporation, the Ford Foundation, and the Lilly Endowment are enabling me to pursue this topic. I appreciate not only the material support but also the interest and encouragement I received from Alden Dunham and Karen Egan at Carnegie, Gladys Chang Hardy and Sheila Biddle at Ford, and Laura Bornholdt at Lilly. Finishing the manuscript was greatly furthered by the award of a sabbatical leave for the academic year 1982–83, for which I am grateful to the University of Massachusetts at Boston. I also want to express my appreciation to several colleagues there, from whose insights and experience I have gained in many conversations. In particular I am grateful to Franklin Patterson and Dorothy Marshall, who not only helped me with their own views but also invited me twice to present papers to the Alden Seminar, which brings together corporate and academic chief executives for intensive discussions. A similar opportunity to present a paper to the American Council on Education Business/Higher Education Forum was also very helpful.

The manuscript for this book benefited from helpful comments by several individuals who had the patience to read it. I am grateful to Dorothy Fenwick at ACE; to David Breneman, then at Brookings; to Robert Craig at ASTD, also for his willingness to write a foreword; to Henry Winkler from Cincinnati; to Kenneth Huddleston from Wisconsin; and to Ed Harris from UMass/Amherst. As the book moved toward publication, Jim Murray at ACE has been patient and supportive. And I am just beginning to realize the value of a meticulous editor through the work of Deirdre Murphy at Macmillan.

It is customary to end acknowledgments with an expression of gratitude to long-suffering family members for bearing with the author through arduous struggles. Fortunately this does not apply, because my wife made my spending much of a sabbatical year working at home a shared pleasure. That calls for more than thanks. Like an earlier book, this volume is dedicated to Carla, for reasons that the years since then have intensified and reconfirmed beyond all imagining. To this dedication I add our sons, infants then, because of the meaning that they since have given to our lives.

Brookline, November 1983   Ernest Lynton

CHAPTER 1

The Importance of Human Resources

The Work Force in Post-Industrial Society

We are living in the post-industrial society. The sociologist
Daniel Bell (1973) was the first to use this term in describing the
characteristics of a new era that is quite different from the preceding industrial age. The symbols of this new society might
well be the computer and the office desk, just as its predecessor
might be exemplified by the smoke stack and the assembly line,
and the agricultural period before that by the plow and the
cobbler's bench. Each of these successive states of our society
differed in the way in which it utilized its human resources. In
the pre-industrial period, the dominant portion of labor was involved in growing food. In 1820, more than 70 percent of this
country's work force was on the farm, and as late as 1880 this
had dropped only to about one half. An excellent description
of the changes in the U.S. work force is given by Ginzberg
(1982). The subsequent industrial age brought mechanization to
farming as well as to the production of goods. A growing
number of workers was needed in the burgeoning factories. At
the same time, agricultural machinery enabled fewer farm

1

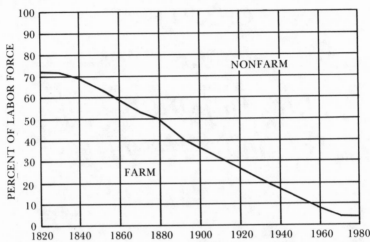

FIGURE 1.1. The Changing Distribution of the U.S. Labor Force between Farm and Non-Farm Occupations, 1820–1980. *Source: Scientific American*—see Ginzberg, 1982.

workers to produce as much and more than had been grown by many more individuals in prior times.

Industrialization was accompanied by the development of a mechanized transportation system, first on rails and later on highways. It led to the growth of cities, and to the consolidation of the production and distribution of goods. These and other factors created an increasing need for services such as transportation and communication, wholesale and retail trade, banks and insurance. As shown in Figure 1.1, by 1920, farm employment had decreased to about one quarter of the total labor force. Figure 1.2 indicates that the workers employed in non-agricultural areas were about equally divided between manufacturing, mining, and construction, on the one hand, and the combined service occupations on the other.

The evolution from the industrial period to the post-industrial society has resulted in further significant changes in employment; these changes are displayed in Figure 1.2. Progress in mechanization and automation has continued to reduce the need for manual labor on the farm, on the factory floor, and in the mine. Agricultual employment has shrunk al-

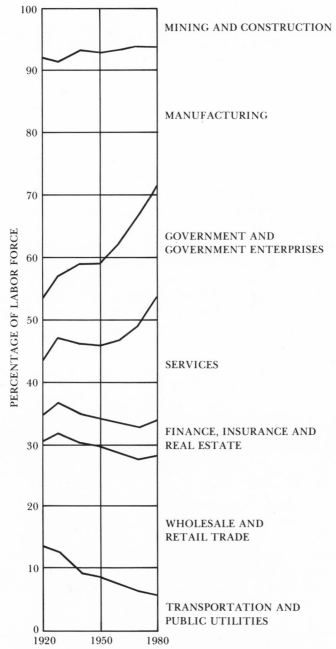

FIGURE 1.2. Changes in the Distribution of the U.S. Labor Force, 1920–1980. *Source: Scientific American—* see Ginzberg, 1982.

most to the vanishing point: it constitutes less than 4 percent of the labor force. Manufacturing, mining, and construction together provide less than 30 percent of all jobs. By contrast, employment in the service sector has increased to about 70 percent of the total. Finance and insurance have continued to grow, as has wholesale and retail trade. Government civil service at local, state, and national levels, as well as other public employment, now adds up to about 20 percent of employment, and a comparable percentage is engaged in the direct delivery of services in fields such as education and health. Ginzberg and Vojta (1981) provide details of the service sector in the U.S. economy.

A further shift in employment pattern within the service sector has been significant in recent years. A growing proportion of individuals are engaged in the production and dissemination of ideas and information. Machlup established the industrial metaphor for this rapidly expanding portion of economic activity through his seminal book *The Production and Distribution of Knowledge in the U.S.* (1962), and Porat (1977) published a nine-volume compendium entitled *The Information Economy*. Both refer to the proliferation of media, the growing number of enterprises providing expert advice, consultation, training, and education, as well as the burgeoning telecommunications and data-processing industries and related activities.

These changes in the American economy can also be characterized by a shift in the contribution of various industrial and business sectors to the national income. Between 1950 and 1981, the share of agriculture decreased from 7.6 to 2.8 percent, and that of manufacturing from 31.3 to 24.1 percent, while those of finance insurance and business services combined rose from 3.2 to 6.9 percent (Cahn, 1983). Table 1.1 lists the contribution from all pertinent sectors.

Within the manufacturing sector as well, significant changes are occurring. The recent recession has, in a paradoxical fashion, both accelerated the pace and obscured the significance of the decline in the "smokestack" industries, such as steel and automobile production. We tend to view the ups and downs of the

TABLE 1.1. Industry Composition of National Income

INDUSTRY	% OF TOTAL NATIONAL INCOME					
	1950	1960	1971	1976	1981
Agriculture	7.6%	4.2%	3.0%	2.9%	2.8%
Mining exc. oil	1.3	0.7	0.5	0.7	0.7
Oil and gas mining	0.8	0.6	0.3	0.8	1.2
Construction	5.0	5.1	5.6	4.9	4.7
Durable manufacturing	17.6	17.4	15.3	15.3	14.3
Nondurable manufacturing	13.7	12.3	10.5	10.6	9.8
Transportation	5.5	4.3	3.8	3.7	3.6
Communication	1.4	2.0	2.1	2.2	2.3
Electric, gas and other utilities	1.6	2.1	1.9	1.9	2.0
Wholesale trade	5.8	5.9	5.8	6.2	6.5
Retail trade	11.0	9.5	9.5	9.0	8.2
Finance, insurance	2.5	3.9	4.2	3.7	4.3
Real estate	6.6	8.0	7.7	7.8	9.2
Business services	0.7	1.3	1.8	2.0	2.6
Health services	1.8	2.5	3.7	4.3	4.7
Other services	6.4	6.8	7.3	7.1	7.2
Federal government	5.2	6.0	6.3	5.4	4.7
State and local government	4.5	6.5	9.6	10.0	9.2
Rest of world	0.7	0.8	1.0	1.5	2.0

Source: Cahn, 1983, based on data from the Bureau of Economic Analysis.

economy as basically cyclical, with recovery inevitably following a downturn. But the malaise of our traditional heavy industry does not appear to be merely temporary. And although most observers anticipate a degree of recovery (see, e.g., Abernathy et al., 1983), this is not likely to lead to the rehiring of all the laid-off automobile workers. Table 1.2 indicates current work-force size as well as projections to 1995 for the automobile industry as well as for some other major manufacturing sectors, and contrasts this with changes in the service sector. It is clear that many workers will have to be trained and redirected if they are to find employment again.

The combination of all of these developments has brought about a marked change in the nature of our work force. There has been a substantial shift in the categories and types of available occupations as employment moved from agriculture and manufacturing to the provision of services, resulting in the need for many new skills. In addition, the content and the required skills for many of the traditional jobs have themselves changed, sometimes out of all recognition as compared to what they were a few years ago. This has happened in all sectors of the economy. Modern technology, and particularly the advent of the microcomputer, has triggered in all of these a rapid mechanization and automation which are bringing about fundamental change in the way in which human labor is used. The September 1982 issue of *Scientific American* contains a series of articles analyzing the impact of modern technology on agriculture (Rasmussen, 1982), mining (Marovelli and Karhnak, 1982), design and manufacturing (Gunn, 1982), commerce (Ernst, 1982), office work (Giuliano, 1982), and women's work (Scott, 1982). All of these analyses illustrate a common trend. The nature of employment is rapidly changing: a growing number of functions require a substantial level of skill and sophistication.

The change in the type of available jobs is perhaps most strikingly illustrated by the fact that between 1900 and 1970, the proportion of professional and managerial positions in the work force increased from about 10 percent to about 25 percent (Gordon, 1974). The increase in skill requirements of

TABLE 1.2.   Employment, in thousands

INDUSTRY	PEAK YEAR Date	PEAK YEAR Work Force	1982	1995 EST.
Manufacturing Sector:				
Agriculture	1956	5,905	3,229	2,772
Food and Tobacco	1955	1,937	1,689	1,447
Apparel and Household Textiles	1963	1,423	1,208	1,126
Chemicals (except fertilizers and pesticides)	1978	1,054	978	884
Automotive	1978	1,021	716	845
Iron and Steel	1957	952	653	566
Paper	1969	713	649	641
Lumber	1955	763	636	664
Service Sector:				
Wholesale and Retail Trade		13,750	22,667	30,249
Medicine, Education, and Nonprofit Organizations		4,336	10,574	13,964
Business Services (legal, accounting, data processing, etc.)		1,875	5,584	9,429
Finance and insurance		2,303	4,069	5,484
Motels and Repair Services		2,462	3,469	4,507
Real Estate		710	1,507	1,848
Entertainment		608	1,098	1,608

Source: Interindustry Forecasting Project, University of Maryland, 1983.

many jobs whose content has changed without acquiring a new label can be seen in the periodic editions of the *Dictionary of Occupational Titles* (DOT) published by the U.S. Employment Service (1977). The dictionary provides estimates of the general skill requirements (General Educational Development—GED) of each occupational title, expressed in terms of a six-point scale of GED levels, with 6 representing the highest skill level (corresponding to graduate training), 4 and 5 to some undergraduate education and college graduation, respectively, down to 1, representing some years of elementary education. An analysis by Rumberger (1979) shows marked increases in levels 4 and 5 for most occupations, offset in part by some decrease in level 6.

These changes in GED levels of many occupations indicate something more than just an increase in necessary skills. They also suggest a change in the nature of these skills. One of the first to point this out was the sociologist Peter Drucker, in his by now classic description of contemporary society entitled *The Age of Discontinuity,* first published in 1968 (Drucker, 1978). Drucker describes the rise of modern industry; he points out that throughout the nineteenth century, industry was largely experience-based rather than knowledge-based, and he defines knowledge as "systematic, purposeful, organized information." A knowledge base is characteristic of the newly emerging industries of our age. As a result, these "embody a new economic reality: knowledge has become the central economic resource. The systematic acquisition of knowledge, that is, organized formal education, has replaced experience—acquired traditionally through apprenticeship—as the foundation for productive capacity and performance" (Drucker, 1978, p. 70). It is therefore not surprising that the change from agricultural to industrial and thence to post-industrial society with its evolving pattern of employment has been accompanied by dramatic increases in formal education. The following are a few illustrative facts:

- The transformation from an agricultural to an industrial society was marked by a large increase in the percentage of the population attending grades 9 through 12. Between 1870 and 1940, enrollment in the elementary grades increased only a little, from 56 to 62 percent of the age group between 5 and 17. By contrast, proportional high school attendance during the same years jumped by a factor of thirty, from 0.7 to 22 percent (*Digest of Educational Statistics,* 1964).

- The change to post-industrial society was marked by a similar growth of enrollment at the post-secondary level. From 1940 until 1980, this increased from 1.5 million to 11.5 million, or from about 10 to almost 40 percent of the 18–24 age group (*Digest of Education Statistics,* 1981; *1981–82 Fact Book for Academic Administrators,* 1981).
- The educational attainment of workers in most job categories has also increased. College graduates dominated high-level white-collar occupations to a much greater extent in 1979 than in 1970, filling an increasing number of professional and technical jobs formerly held by persons with only a high school diploma. Even more significant is the rise in educational attainment in other job categories. For example, in 1970, more than 60 percent of blue-collar workers had not graduated from high school and only one in twenty had one or more years of college. By 1979, 44 percent were high school graduates and the proportion of those with some college education had more than doubled (Young, 1981).
- The Bureau of Labor Statistics compiled a study in June 1982 (BLS, 1982) showing the median school years completed among the entire work force to be more than twelve years. Between 1950 and 1982, the percentage of individuals in the work force with four years of college or more increased from about 7% to over 20%, 36% had completed at least one year (Young, 1981; 1983).

The overall changes in the educational attainment of the U.S. work force are summarized in Figure 1.3, which compares 1957 with 1978. During that period, the median number of school years completed by members of the civilian labor force increased from 10.6 to 12.6 years. By 1978, one out of three workers had at least attended college, and one out of six had a college degree (Ginzberg and Vojta, 1981).

The meaning of these and many similar facts about the

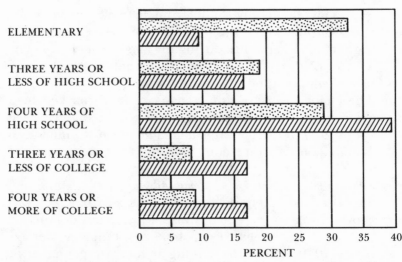

ELEMENTARY

THREE YEARS OR
LESS OF HIGH SCHOOL

FOUR YEARS OF
HIGH SCHOOL

THREE YEARS OR
LESS OF COLLEGE

FOUR YEARS OR
MORE OF COLLEGE

0   5   10   15   20   25   30   35   40

PERCENT

FIGURE 1.3. Changes in Educational Attainment of the U.S. Civilian Labor Force between 1957 (upper bars) and 1978 (lower bars). *Source: Scientific American*—see Ginzberg and Vojta, 1981.

changing nature of our work force has been much debated in recent years. Some observers believe that the steady rise in educational attainment is not reflected in corresponding increases in intrinsic job content and skill requirements. This will be discussed further later in this chapter. It should also be noted that not all jobs in this post-industrial age are subject to such a steady increase in educational requirements. In fact, while the fastest percentage growth in employment has been in high-skill areas such as data processing, computers, and office machinery, the largest increase in *absolute* numbers has been within the ranks of janitors, hospital nurses' aids and orderlies, and fast food clerks (Levin and Rumberger, 1983). This is shown in Table 1.3. Occupations such as these are characterized not only by their low skill levels but also by the fact that they are dead-end jobs, leading nowhere. Unlike in the past, when a combination of hard work and on-the-job experience enabled individuals to work their way up from almost any starting positions, we now appear to have entered an age in which there is a marked discontinuity of education and skills between a large number of

TABLE 1.3. Employment and Employment Growth in the Fastest Growing Occupations: 1978–90

	EMPLOYMENT GROWTH 1978–90				
	Employment (thousands)			Number of Jobs	
OCCUPATIONS	1978	1990	Percentage Increase	(thousands)	(% of all occupations)
Fastest relative growth[a]					
1. Data processing machine mechanics	63	156	148	93	0.4
2. Paralegal	28	66	132	38	0.2
3. Computer systems analysts	185	384	108	199	0.9
4. Computer operators	169	317	88	148	0.7
5. Office machine and cash register servicers	49	89	81	40	0.2
Total	494	1012	105	518	2.4
Fastest absolute growth[b]					
1. Janitors and sextons	2585	3257	26	672	3.1
2. Nurses/aides and orderlies	1089	1683	55	594	2.7
3. Sales clerks	2771	3362	21	591	2.7
4. Cashiers	1501	2046	36	545	2.5
5. Waiters/Waitresses	1539	2071	35	532	2.4
Total	9485	12419	31	2934	13.3

[a]Based on the percentage increase in the number of jobs created.
[b]Based on the number of new jobs created.
Source: Levin and Rumberger, 1983, based on Carey, 1981.

entry-level jobs and any kind of upward mobility. This further reinforces the importance of providing adequate educational opportunities, lest we create a quasi-permanent underclass that lacks the qualifications for any work other than at the lowest level (Carnevale, 1982, p. 110).

Some observers of recent developments are voicing a second warning with regard to the impact of technology. They believe that mechanization might make many occupations increasingly repetitive and routinized, and thus require fewer rather than more sophisticated skills (see Levin and Rumberger, 1983). We shall return to this issue in a later chapter.

An additional debate revolves around the question of whether technological advances merely shift the nature of the work force without appreciably reducing overall employment, or whether these advances will result in a net decrease in overall labor requirements. Leontieff (1982) points out that when workers are displaced by machines, the economy may suffer from the loss of their purchasing power and from the social charges imposed by their unemployment. This may create the need for shortening the work week or developing other ways of sharing work. The use of educational leave to spread jobs and to reduce unemployment has been proposed by Emmerij (1982) and others.

These serious issues notwithstanding, there appears to be general agreement about the basic fact that our contemporary, post-industrial society requires a substantial proportion of highly skilled and well-educated workers. The development as well as the maintenance of human resources capable of much more than physical labor has become essential to the economy's vitality. Quite recently, there has been a veritable flood of statements, articles, and books all making this point. They call variously for more support for education, greater accountability, or higher standards. A strong statement of the importance of technically and scientifically trained manpower for the maintenance of this country's lead in high technology is contained in a recent book, *Global Stakes,* co-authored by the chief executive of a high-technology corporation. It advocates "investment in people" and describes this as:

the codeword for a new economic outlook where human
resources, with their stock of information, education,
and knowledge, become the key resource and where
human ingenuity, to learn, innovate, and communicate,
becomes the key to increasing productivity and society's
standard of living. Also, it is retraining and reeducation
to keep our work force abreast of changing technology,
and to accomodate transitions from sunset to sunrise industries. [Botkin et al., 1982, p. 24]

Similar points are made in a series of essays on the contribution of higher education to the economy of New England,
published recently by the New England Board of Higher Education (Hoy and Bernstein, 1981; 1982a; 1982b).

The growing importance of the nature and skills of the
work force is also indicated by studies of the labor market imbalance carried out by Medoff (1982). He has looked at the relationship between unemployment and indicators of job vacancies. In a balanced labor market, one would expect vacancies to
decrease as unemployment increases. Instead, Medoff observed
that after 1975, unemployment and vacancies *both* tended to
increase. This shows that although there were many individuals
without jobs, there also existed a large number of jobs for
which there were no individuals qualified to fill them.

The emphasis on retraining and reeducation in the statement quoted above from *Global Stakes* is particularly appropriate. What is at the forefront today can rapidly slip back. New
England's cotton mills and shoe factories were the high technology around the turn of the century. Two decades later, Henry
Ford placed the automobile industry at the technological
forefront through the development of the assembly line. In
turn, today's high technology will be overtaken by newer developments and newer products, requiring not only new equipment and plants, but also—and in increasing measure—new
skills and insights on the part of the employees.

Indeed, the continuing vitality of almost every component
of our economy depends on its ability to *assimilate* technological
innovations. New scientific breakthroughs, new inventions, and

new techniques are necessary, but they are not sufficient by themselves to ensure continuing economic development. The innovations must be absorbed into the fabric of the economy if productivity and competitiveness are to be enhanced. The skills of the labor force will have to keep pace with accelerating technological change. This has been very clearly stated by Carnevale:

> As the pace of technological change accelerates, our ability to *adapt* our human skills to the new technologies and to *integrate* new production techniques with available labor will be critical. Adaptation will be all the more difficult as product life and skill life become shorter and shorter. Moreover, it is ultimately the *rate* at which we apply new technologies and integrate them with a ready labor force that will determine our success. [1982, p. 110]

The same point is made by Reich (1983). He calls for a major transformation of American industry from the existing emphasis on high-volume, standardized production to what he calls "flexible-system production" which concentrates on precision products, custom products, and technology-driven products. This transition "requires a massive change in the skills of American labor, requiring investments in human capital beyond the capacity of any individual firm" (Reich, 1983, p. 133).

Both Carnevale and Reich stress that the importance of enhancing the skills of our work force is further increased by the rapid trend toward what economists call "rationalization of labor" on a global scale. The rise of multinational corporations and a general relaxation of trade barriers since the Second World War is leading to a sorting out of categories of enterprises among types of countries. Activity characterized by relatively higher technology, higher wages, and higher productivity becomes concentrated in the more developed countries while lower-wage, lower-skill, and lower-productivity work uses the large pools of unskilled labor in the less developed countries (Carnevale, 1982, p. 113; Reich, 1983, p. 125).

All of this leads to the inescapable conclusion that the economic well-being of our society depends in large measure on providing a high level of knowledge and skills to substantial segments of the work force. In addition, it is equally evident that the necessary proficiencies are not static, but highly dynamic. They require continuous and systematic updating by appropriate education in order to keep pace with accelerating technological and societal change.

Human Capital Theory

The basic premise of this book is that the development as well as the maintenance of highly educated and skilled human resources are of great economic importance to this country and should represent a shared concern of educators and employers. The nature and the extent of the societal and the individual returns on investment in education have been the subject of much study and an almost equal amount of disagreement during the past twenty years. Human capital theory looks both at the relationship between the educational attainment of the work force and the economic strength and level of productivity of the country, as well as at the impact of such attainment on the income of an individual. Correlations at both the societal and the individual levels are readily established, but some critics question the extent to which the correlation indeed reflects a causal relationship.

As far back as Adam Smith, economists have pointed to the economic benefits of education. However, the issue was not approached quantitatively until about 1960. One of the first attempts was that of Denison (1962), who tried to identify the proportion of the growth of real national income that was due to the increased skills of the work force. Unable to measure this directly, he used a so-called "residue" approach: subtracting the growth due to all other identifiable sources, such as physical capital investment, Denison found a substantial residue which he attributed to the impact of education. In his later work he concluded that increased education of workers in the business

TABLE 1.4. Sources of U.S. Economic Growth, 1929–1969, in Percentages of Average Annual Growth Rate

	1929–1969	1948–1969
Potential national income	100.0	100.0
Advances in knowledge and changes not elsewhere classified	31.1	34.1
More work done, with account taken of the characteristics of workers except education	28.7	23.9
More physical capital	15.8	21.6
Increased Education per Worker	14.1	11.9
Improved resource allocation	10.0	9.0
Dwelling occupancy ratio and irregular factors	0.3	−0.5

Source: Denison, 1974, p. 130. Copyright © 1974 The Brookings Institute.

sector contributed about 14 percent of the U.S. economic growth during the period 1929–1969, while adding almost 25 percent to the potential output per worker (Denison, 1974). His figures are shown in Table 1.4.

Expanding on this, Carnevale (1983) has recently published summary data indicating that the principal contributions to productivity in recent years have been the combination of "working smarter" and "education." By "working smarter," Carnevale means process improvements that are due to the assimilation of education, training, and on-the-job experience into production. His conclusions are displayed graphically in Figure 1.4.

In parallel with efforts to obtain a measure of the impact of education on productivity came the development of a quantitative approach to the concept of "human capital." Economists define this in a manner completely analogous to the notion of physical capital: an aggregate of assets that leads to the production of goods and services. Physical capital consists of items such as land, raw materials, factories, and machinery. By analogy, human capital includes the skills of workers and the abilities of managers, together with a variety of factors that further contribute to the productive potential of individuals, such as health and information about and ready access to job opportunities.

FIGURE 1.4. Components of Growth in Economic Output 1948–1978 and Projected through 1990. *Source:* Carnevale, 1983, p. 43.

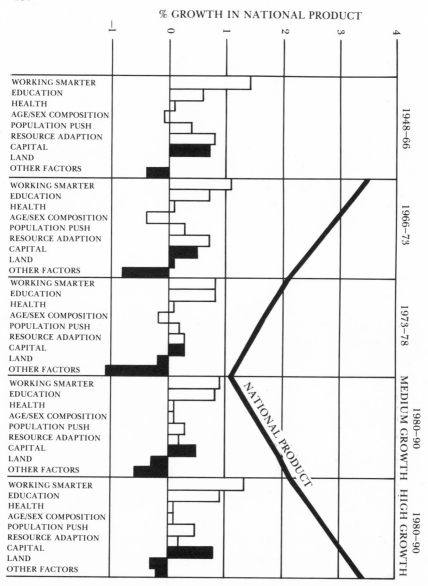

The groundwork for a systematic assessment of a nation's stock of human capital was laid particularly by the economist Schultz at the University of Chicago (Schultz, 1961; 1963). Concurrently, his colleague Becker (1960; 1964), and others, initiated what became an increasingly sophisticated attempt to measure the return on investment in human capital formation. Wykstra (1971) has edited an informative set of articles by some of the principal human capital theorists. Douglass (1977) and McPherson (1982) provide excellent overviews of the development of the theories. Critiques of their content are summarized by Clecak (1977).

Douglass (1977) points out that "the most remarkable feature of the concept of human capital is its narrowness in relation to the totality of human life" (p. 363). The theories are characterized by a conscious exclusion of all non-monetary consequences of education and focus solely on material returns. This is true for the attempts to measure private returns, which take into account only anticipated lifetime earnings as the sole measure of an individual's benefit from learning. Similarly, all quantitative work on the social or public returns on investment in human capital looks only at material indicators such as gross national income or product, productivity, and the like. Intangibles that cannot be quantified are omitted from detailed analyses, although of course they are also very important in assessing the value of education. In *Investment in Learning*, Bowen (1978) discusses both individual and social goals of education. Among the former he includes cognitive learning, emotional and moral development, and practical competence, as well as direct satisfaction and enjoyment. Social goals include the advancement of knowledge, the discovery and encouragement of talent, and the advancement of social welfare. Many of these cannot be measured or analyzed quantitatively, yet all of them contribute significantly to the returns on the investment in learning.

McPherson (1983) similarly observes that there are non-economic as well as economic aspects of education. He points out that Dewey and others have always stressed that "the calling forth of a person's capacities for practical activity, in both their intellectual and affective dimension, cannot meaningfully be decomposed into 'vocational' and 'liberal' components" (p. 253). McPherson further reminds us that Schultz, Nobel prize laureate and dean of the human capital school of economists, has repeatedly stressed the non-quantifiable elements of this form of capital. In particular, Schultz considers the ability to deal with disequilibria to be a key component of the value of human capital. He suggests that education is important because it strengthens an individual's capacities to perceive and to respond to change.

Clearly, therefore, those calculated rates of return on investment in education that consider only quantifiable aspects are likely to underestimate the totality of benefits, and thus constitute a minimum value. Thus, regardless of specific quantitative details, one can accept the principal conclusion of human capital theory: it established the cost of education as what economists call "investment expenditures" rather than as "consumption expenditures." An investment expenditure constitutes a commitment of resources with a reasonable expectation of positive return. This clearly applies to expenditures for education, and one can in fact conclude with Douglass (1977), that "economically, education is a good investment" (p. 387).

Douglass makes this statement primarily with regard to the social or public returns, and few critics would disagree. There is much less agreement as to whether education constitutes a good individual investment. The issue is, of course, raised only with regard to post-compulsory (and therefore, on the whole, higher) education. During the boom years of the late sixties, research on this issue showed substantial differences in lifetime earnings between college graduates and individuals with only a high school education (see, for example, Douglass, 1977, p. 364). However, during the past decade, employment opportunities declined even for college degree holders, particularly in some areas such as teaching. This resulted in growing fear of "overeducation" and triggered a number of books with quite alarming titles, such as *The Overeducated American* (Freeman, 1976), *The Case against College* (Bird, 1975), and *The Great Training Robbery* (Berg, 1970). The cab driver with a Ph.D. became a kind of national symbol of the persisting situation in which many college graduates have no employment at all or are in jobs with substantially lower education requirements. Similar problems exist in other countries (see, for example, Dore, 1976).

Yet the recent economic downturn has also indicated very clearly that although an advanced degree does not ensure a job, it significantly enhances the probability of one. Figures published by the Bureau of Labor Statistics show an unemployment rate in March 1982 of 3.0 percent for college graduates, as compared with 8.5 percent for those with only a high school diploma, 12.1 percent for those with one to three years of high school, and 13.2 percent for persons with only elementary school. There also is greater stability in the jobs held by college graduates even during recessions (BLS, 1982; Young, 1983; see also Carnegie Council, 1980).

In addition to questions regarding the validity of looking at lifetime earnings as a measure of the value of education, a quite different category of criticism of human capital theory has been raised by a number of scholars on social and ideological grounds. Rumberger (1982) and Clecak (1977) recently summarized much of this work. Berg (1970) was among the first to point out that economists working on the theory ask no questions either about the content or the quality of the education, on the one hand, or about the intrinsic educational requirements of the jobs, on the other hand. Educational attainment is measured only in terms of attendance, and neither hiring practices nor levels of remuneration are tested against the skills and knowledge that are really needed for a job. Berg, among others, believes that on the whole jobs have not changed in terms of their difficulty and complexity at the same rate as the educational requirements used by employers in filling these jobs. According to these critics, the increasing educational requirements imposed by employers in their recruitment of personnel reflect a growing credentialism which is used as a screening device and tends to reinforce social and economic stratification.

There are observers who see this as a deliberate policy to

maintain the class differences essential to a capitalist society (Bowles and Gintis, 1976). Some critics have gone so far as to recommend the complete abolition of all formal schooling (Illich, 1971). A more benign interpretation describes a quasi-automatic "market credentialism" in which social and historical forces result in increasing educational levels (Rawlings and Ulman, 1974). According to the latter view, employers always hire at the highest available level both because it is the safest approach for the manager making the employment decision, and because it provides a pool of individuals from which a few can be selected for ascent through the corporate hierarchy. In an attempt to assess the various contributing elements, Adkins (1974) distinguishes between "technogenic" and "sociogenic" factors determining educational requirements for various occupations. The former are the increased skills intrinsically required by technological and other developments; the latter are due to external factors. Adkins concludes that the role of both factors is significant.

The final word about these controversies has not yet been written, but there appears to be a substantial degree of consensus that technogenic factors are both real and important. They are probably, however, reinforced by sociogenic elements. Furthermore, there is little evidence that either educators or employers have given a great deal of thought to matching educational content with the intrinsic skill requirements of a job. In fact, as the debates with regard to human capital theories wax and wane, two points emerge with growing clarity:

The first of these is that *our contemporary economy indeed requires a highly skilled labor force.* It seems reasonable to accept the basic premise that "The theory of the production contribution of education remains plausible even if the attempts to measure the contribution have not had convincing results" (Machlup, 1970, p. 15). Drucker's statement regarding the replacement of apprenticeship by organized formal education, quoted earlier, makes the same point. It follows directly from this premise that the cost of the necessary education of the labor force represents a substantial investment that can be justified, but must then also be protected and maintained. A later chapter will concentrate on this issue in more detail.

The second point that emerges from a survey of the literature on human capital is *the clear need to go beyond the current practice of looking only at the quantity of education.* It has become essential also to examine its nature and quality. There is no justification for extrapolating from statements regarding the importance of education to an uncritical acceptance of the appropriateness of any kind of education, regardless of content, timing, and approach. In higher education, we have tended to ignore indications of a substantial mismatch between what, when, and how we teach, on the one hand, and the requirements and expectations of the work place on the other. We have failed to reflect on the potential consequences of the inappropriate utilization of college-trained manpower in terms of the dissatisfaction and frustration of the individual. We have given little thought to the extent to which educational requirements can be misused, consciously or not, to reinforce existing social and economic differences. We have paid too little attention to the clear signs that the employers of our graduates harbor an ominous level of dissatisfaction with the outcomes of our educational programs and that we are facing growing competition to which they will turn more and more if we do not change. And, in general, we have not examined the implications of the fact that if human capital is indeed to be viewed as an investment, it requires systematic and ongoing maintenance and renovation.

In short, there has not been enough examination of the educational implications of our changing economy beyond taking the rather simplistic position that education is a good thing and the more of it, the better. Much too little attention has been paid to date on how good a job is being done by the educational institutions that should bear the principal responsibility for the development of human capital and fill at least a substantial role in its recurrent renewal.

Later chapters will further examine the current content and quality of professional education, focusing on three principal aspects:

- The urgent need to recognize that competence transcends knowledge, and that in higher education we must do more to narrow the gap between the abstract and compartmentalized methodologies of separate disciplines on the one hand, and the definition and resolution of complex and messy problems as found in the real world on the other.

- The equally important and fundamental issue that the artificial distinction between "liberal" and "vocational" must be abandoned, and that higher education in close collaboration with its external constituencies must evolve the broad and integrated approach essential for true effectiveness on the job and also as a citizen.
- Last, but certainly not least, the growing necessity to view professional development as a lifelong and recurrent process that needs to be considered in its entirety with optimal coherence and relationship between successive phases.

These and related issues must be faced by higher education with great urgency, because it is faced by real danger. Again the situation has been described dramatically by Drucker, who writes: "Demand for education is actually going up, not down. What is going down, and fairly fast, is demand for traditional education in traditional schools" (Drucker, 1981). Similar apocalyptic statements are being made with increasing frequency by other observers of higher education.

Drucker's position is an overstatement. Enrollment in colleges and universities has not yet decreased. Of course, it will do so in the immediate future because there will be far fewer young people of traditional college age. But there is no indication that the college-going percentage of this age group is declining. However, it is very obvious that demand for "traditional education in traditional schools" does not by any measure reflect the overall growth in demand for training and education. Those new needs are mostly being met by sources outside of the traditional educational system. One of the most striking and—at least to someone in higher education—alarming examples of this is illustrated by the recent growth in employer-sponsored education and training. This will be examined in the subsequent chapters.

CHAPTER 2

Employer-Sponsored Education

Scope and Organization

Employer-sponsored education and training consists of formal instructional activities, as distinct from on-the-job training, that are specifically organized or contracted by employers for a group of employees from one or more enterprises. The rapid growth of these activities constitutes a major educational phenomenon which has only recently received systematic attention. Instruction may be provided by corporate staff, by consultants hired by the employer, or under contract by an educational institution or third-party providers. It may take place on site, on a campus, or elsewhere, and it may vary in length from a few hours to several weeks. In content, it can range from narrowly defined training that focuses on some specific skill or operation, to education about relatively broad and general topics. The next chapter will discuss the nature and content in greater detail and explore possible distinctions between training and education. This chapter describes the scope, organization, and sources of the activities that are subsumed under the label of employer-sponsored education.

Instructional programs for employees are not a new phe-

25

nomenon. As far back as 1913, a sufficient number of company schools existed to lead to the creation of an organization called the National Association of Corporate Schools. These schools focused on vocational training, together with the equivalent of an elementary school curriculum in basic skills. They were limited in size and scope (see Fisher, 1967). The primary method of worker education then and for several subsequent decades continued to be apprenticeship and on-the-job training. Only in more recent years has the private sector seen the need to replace this with a substantial system of formal education and training programs (see Craig and Evers, 1981; Lynton, 1981a, b; 1982a).

This change went largely unnoticed until the mid-seventies when it was described in an article written by two senior executives of IBM for a special issue of *Daedalus* devoted to American higher education (Branscomb and Gilmore, 1975). The authors indicated the scope of education in private industry by citing figures from their own company and from the Bell system. They explained these developments as a reflection of rising concern in American industrial circles over "the intellectual vitality and . . . flexibility of industrial personnel" and pointed out that "An accelerating pace of social and technological change calls for some form of continuing education for which our colleges and universities are not yet organized" (p. 222). This and subsequent portions of their article raised serious questions about the role of higher education in maintaining the effectiveness of the industrial work force. Similar concerns were expressed at about the same time by John Dunlop, then U.S. Secretary of Labor (Dunlop, 1975). He coined the term "shadow system of education" to draw attention to the emergence of a major employer-sponsored complex of instruction which existed in virtual isolation and with little attention from the established academic institutions. Unfortunately, few people in higher education were listening to these clear calls for action.

The full extent of employer-sponsored education was brought home by the first quantitative study, carried out for the Conference Board by Lusterman (1977). The resulting report, published in 1977 and entitled *Education in Industry,* left little doubt of the existence of a major educational enterprise in which colleges and universities were (and still are) but little involved. The study was based on a survey of 610 corporations with 500 or more employees, and combined a lengthy questionnaire with personal interviews. The results clearly indicated that companies increasingly view "education and training as a subsystem of the larger system for assuring the presence of skilled and productive human resources." Lusterman reported that, as a result, "industry is, in fact, no less a segment of the nation's educational system than our colleges and universities, technical institutes, and other schools" (p. 3).

More recent work, some of which is cited later in this book, has superseded some of the quantitative elements of the Lusterman study. In particular, the prevailing information indicates far more considerable corporate expenditures than Lusterman reported. But the Conference Board report remains not only the seminal but also the definitive qualitative description of education in the private sector.

The wide variety of programs that fall into the category of employer-sponsored education and the many different ways in which it can be organized and administered within the broad range of businesses make it extremely difficult to obtain reliable quantitative information about the current scope of this activity. Attempts to do so have to rely either on information supplied by the employer or on surveys of employees.

The reliability of data obtained from employers is limited by a number of factors. Corporate accounting systems are highly inconsistent in their treatment of training costs. Most businesses treat training as a discretionary expense and do not break it down as a separately budgeted item. Decisions about resources allocated to training are usually very decentralized with little or no oversight and accounting on a companywide basis. In assessing costs, some enterprises count only direct expenditures, such as trainer or consultant salaries, instructional materials, and the like. Others include some overhead costs such as space and utilities. A very few also attempt to include the opportunity costs represented by the salaries and wages of those who are being trained and therefore absent from their jobs. There is further inconsistency as to what is to be included as employee training and development. For example, certain types of activities related to organizational development are considered as part of this category in some companies and not in others (see Craig, 1983; Anderson, 1983).

This lack of uniformity not only prevents the generation of precise data with regard to total costs of employer-sponsored training, but also prevents any systematic comparison of the practices and expenditures of different employers. While it can be argued that it is not very useful to know the total expenditures in employer-sponsored education with great precision, the ability to make comparisons is important both as a way of arriving at some measure of return on investment and also to provide some normative guidelines for management.

Individual information about involvement in employee education is, in principle, available from the Current Population Survey (CPS) carried out by the Bureau of the Census. This is a monthly operation which, starting in 1969, has included a Survey of Participation in Adult Education every three years. In each of 58,000 households, one individual is interviewed and asked whether any adult in the household has taken any courses or training during the preceding twelve months. Information is collected for each person involved in such activities: what courses were taken, where they were given, who paid for them, and the reason for taking them. The results of the 1981 survey, as published by the National Center for Education Statistics (Kay, 1982), show that of the 37 million course enrollments by more than 21 million adults, employers in all categories—public and private—paid for about 12 million. Of these, more than 9 million enrollments were in courses actually provided by the employer. The remaining 3 million were in courses offered by educational institutions and other sources (Kay, 1982, pp. 14, 15). It is interesting to note that of the 12 million course enrollments funded by the employer, 54 percent were taken by men and only 46 percent by women, whereas women constituted almost 60 percent of enrollment in the sum total of adult education. This may well be because the majority of employer-sponsored programs is provided for the higher echelons of the work force in which women are proportionally underrepresented.

The usefulness of the CPS information, however, is also limited. There is every reason to believe that the results severely underestimate adult participation in education generally, and also the specific component sponsored by employers. The one individual interviewed in each household is not necessarily familiar with the on-the-job activities of all other members, particularly with regard to short instructional activities such as daylong workshops. Furthermore, the household surveys, of course, provide no information at all with regard to costs, except for direct payments by individuals. Thus, even if a survey supplied accurate data as to total amount of employer-sponsored training, the expenditures for this could only be estimated on the basis of some plausible range of unit cost (Goldstein, 1983; Tierney, 1983).

The reasons for the lack of reliable quantitative data on employer-sponsored education go beyond the complexity and heterogeneity of the delivery system and the ambiguity of cost definition. As Weinstein (1982) points out: "training is not considered by employers to be a primary function of the organization.... [It] is judged to be peripheral...a low priority need...to be done only when absolutely necessary. Further, costs were assumed to be so minimal that no one thought to keep a record of them" (p. 263). Anderson (1983) reinforces this by noting the absence of management interest in measuring outcomes of employee development. He concludes that "Cost information is useful only if it can be coupled with benefits.... if there are no decisions to be made, there are no reasons to collect information" (p. 3). A later chapter will return to the evident ambivalences in employer attitudes toward the role and importance of human resource development.

Even though precise data are not available, enough is known about employer-sponsored activities to provide a good estimate of its current scope. The most widely accepted figure puts the total direct expenditures in the range of $20 to $40 billion per year (Craig and Evers, 1981). This does not include indirect costs incurred by the sponsoring enterprise, nor does it allow for the value of lost employee time. If these two substantial factors were included, the total yearly cost would rise to at least twice the direct expenditures (Weinstein, 1982).

Thus, these activities comprise, in their aggregate, a developmental system of considerable magnitude. One obtains a sense of its importance by comparing the above-cited figures with operating budgets of traditional institutions of higher education. In 1981–1982, for example, the sum total of all state appropriations for colleges and universities added up to $22.6 billion, which included almost $1 billion for student aid (see, for example, Beal, 1982). These funds pay for almost all of the direct instructional activities of public institutions and also provide, in some states, institutional support for the private sector. Federal support for higher education is primarily in the form of student financial aid and research grants and contracts. Thus, it is evident that the scope of the "shadow system" is comparable to the aggregate of the state-funded instructional activities of all public higher education in the United States.

One can obtain some further measures of the size of this system by a few representative facts:

- Drucker (1973) states that in the 1940s, only a single corporation in the United States and one in Great Britain conducted management programs. A decade later, already, there were more than 3,000, and by now the number has grown further.
- An extensive U.S. Training Census and Trends Report states that among enterprises with more than fifty employees, almost 60 percent have at least one full-time individual engaged in training and development (Zemke, 1983; the report is based on a survey of over 1,700 enterprises with 50 or more employees. It has been summarized in the October 1982 issue of *Training*). As shown in Table 2.1, the total number of full-time trainers in the United States is about 213,000, with an additional 786,000 engaged in training on a part-time basis.
- All but the smallest and largest enterprises employ, on the average, one full-time trainer for every few hundred employees (Zemke, 1983).

TABLE 2.1. Number and Distribution of Trainers in Organizational America

Organization Size, by Number of Employees	Avg. Number of Full-Time Trainers	Avg. Number of Part-Time Trainers	Est. Number of Full-Time Trainers in U.S.	Est. Number of Part-Time Trainers in U.S.
50–99	1.9	14.0	30,575	224,515
100–499	3.8	13.5	97,768	341,090
500–999	3.5	6.1	20,070	35,183
1,000–2,499	5.7	18.8	23,239	76,528
2,500–9,999	9.7	94.7	7,430	75,528
10,000–24,000	37.5	26.6	23,513	16,667
25,000+	53.4	85.3	12,282	19,616
			212,877	786,127

Source: Zemke, 1983, p. 8. Reprinted with permission from the *U.S. Training Census and Trends Report*, 1982–83. Copyright 1983, Lakewood Publications, Inc., Minneapolis, MN (612)333-0471. All rights reserved.

- The Bell System alone, with about 1 million employees, spends more than $1 billion each year on its training efforts, including about $100 million each on the development or revision of programs and on research in learning and training (Blount, 1980). The employee participation rate is about 40 percent, as compared with a 13 percent average for all companies in the Lusterman study. It passes about 10,000 employees each year through its Center for Technical Education in Lisle, Illinois, for two-to-three-week intensive programs (Luxenberg, 1978/1979), employs about 10,000 trainers (Zemke, 1983, p. 11), and provides about 12,000 courses in 1,300 locations for 20,000–30,000 employees *every day* (ASTD, 1980).
- The American Society for Training and Development (ASTD), the principal professional association for trainers, has grown to about 50,000 members in recent years.

However, while these "gee-whiz" numbers clearly indicate that employer-sponsored training adds up to a considerable system of human resource development, it is still quite limited both in terms of the amount of instruction provided to any one individual and in terms of the percentage and the categories of participating employees.

Both the Lusterman survey (1977, p. 49) and the more recent Training Report (Zemke, 1983, p. 18) indicate that less than one-third of the participating companies provided as much as thirty hours of courses per year to *any* group of employees. This group is most likely to consist of professionals, supervisors, or sales representatives. Moreover, the entire system of employer-sponsored education displays a pervasive imbalance with regard to the participation of categories of employees. The managerial levels are much more likely to receive structured instruction than are the lower ranks. General office personnel and production workers are least likely to receive any training at all. This is indicated very clearly by Table 2.2. The contrast between the upper six levels and the other four categories is striking. For the latter, it is twice as likely that structured training will be provided rarely or not at all.

TABLE 2.2. Frequency and Location of Training

Job Role	Rarely Structured Training	Receives Training In-House	Receives Most Training at Outside Seminar Wkshps.	Receives Both In-House and Outside Training	Amount	
					Over 30 Hours	Under 30 Hours
Executives (Policy-level mgrs.)	27.4%	7.1	32.7	32.9	24.9	75.1
Senior Managers (top-level, non-policy)	19.6	11.8	25.7	42.9	28.2	71.8
Middle Managers	12.7	22.5	14.0	50.8	31.9	68.1
First-Line Supervisors/Foremen	14.1	45.7	4.3	35.9	36.7	63.3
Sales Reps	24.1	34.9	10.3	30.8	35.6	64.4
Professionals (engineers, scientists, nurses)	16.1	14.8	23.7	45.3	39.4	60.4
Administrative Employees	38.3	30.9	9.1	21.7	13.1	86.9
Office/Secretarial General Clerical	44.6	33.2	6.2	16.0	13.8	86.0
Production Workers	40.9	43.1	2.8	13.1	25.3	74.7
Customer Service	37.6	45.1	3.9	13.9	21.1	78.9

Source: Zemke, 1983, p. 18. Reprinted with permission from the *U.S. Training Census and Trends Report*, 1982–83. Copyright 1983, Lakewood Publications, Inc., Minneapolis, MN (612)333-0471. All rights reserved.

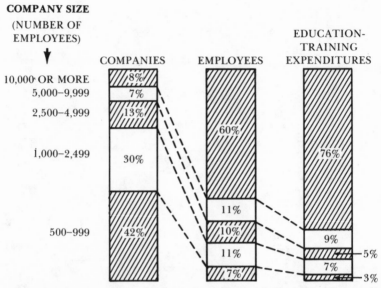

FIGURE 2.1. Employees and Education and Training Expenditures in Companies of Various Size. *Source:* Lusterman, 1977, p. 17.

Systematic training and development programs for employees are most prevalent in larger companies. Lusterman reports that corporations employing more than 10,000 individuals represent 60 percent of the labor force but provide 76 percent of the expenditures for employee training. This is shown in Figure 2.1. By contrast, enterprises with between 500 and 1,000 employees account for 3 percent of the total expenditures, even though they account for 7 percent of the total force. The Training Survey shows that of organizations with 100 to 500 individuals on the payroll, more than 20 percent have no one on their staff with even part-time training responsibilities. As indicated in Table 2.3, that figure rises to above 40 percent for businesses in the 50–100-employee range. On the other hand, all but 2 or 3 percent of enterprises with more than 500 employees have at least one person charged with training activities. This amounts to a very serious gap in the availability of employer-sponsored education. Companies with less than 500 employees constitute more than 90 percent of all enterprises and in the aggregate employ more than 50 percent of the labor force (BLS, 1982).

The organizational patterns of employer-sponsored development programs vary quite widely. There appears to be a growing emphasis on the principle of managerial accountability for education and training. Lusterman (1977) quotes one industry executive as saying that "Employee development is now recognized in our company as no less a responsibility of individual managers than productivity or accident rates" (p. 27). As a result, decisions as to what programs are needed and who should participate are increasingly made at the local, decentralized level. At the same time, however, one also finds a growing incidence of central training departments. In a few cases, these are solely responsible for all in-house programs. More often, central departments are there to provide advice and technical assistance to decentralized training units or to individual managers, and also to organize certain companywide activities. Some major corporations have appointed a senior staff person to advise top management on human resource development needs and to oversee and evaluate ongoing activities.

T A B L E 2.3. Proportion of Organizations Reporting No and at Least One Full-Time Trainer

ORGANIZATION SIZE BY NUMBER OF EMPLOYEES	NO EMPLOYEE WITH TRAINING RESPONSIBILITY	AT LEAST ONE FULL-TIME TRAINER IN ORGANIZATION
50–99	42.9	16.1
100–499	21.0	30.9
500–999	3.9	62.1
1,000–2,499	3.7	82.6
2,500–9,999	2.8	85.3
10,000–24,999	0.0	91.7
25,000+	0.0	94.1
Full Sample	19.3	57.7

Source: Zemke, 1983, p. 6. Reprinted with permission from the *U.S. Training Census and Trends Report,* 1982–83. Copyright 1983, Lakewood Publications, Inc., Minneapolis, MN (612)333-0471. All rights reserved.

Sources

Information about the sources of employer-sponsored programs, like its cost estimates, suffers from inadequate data and
is only qualitatively reliable. Among the companies participating in the Lusterman survey, all of which had 500 or more employees, 80 percent of expenditures were for "company
courses" specifically provided for and limited to the employees
of the firm. However, the survey provides no further breakdown as to what proportion of these courses are designed and
conducted by company personnel or by consultants, and what
part is provided under contract by an educational institution or
by some other category of third-party vendor. Of the 20 percent of expenditures for what Lusterman classifies as "outside"
courses, about one-half represents tuition reimbursement for
employees taking courses of their own choice and not specifically designed for their purposes. The other half of the remaining expenditures, approximately 9 percent of the total, is for
courses that are taken by employees in the line of duty and at
the behest of their employers, but are open to participants other than employees of a particular company. This last category
includes the special programs developed by many colleges and
universities for managers and executives, as well as courses
provided by special corporate suppliers, professional and
trade groups, and proprietary organizations.

Lusterman's figures on sources of employee education are
consistent with those of the Training Report, according to
which:
- 61.5 percent of responding enterprises use their own staff
  to design, develop, and deliver most training;
- 51.3 percent buy or lease pre-packaged training programs;
- 46.8 percent bring in training and development consultants to design and/or deliver programs.

The numbers add up to more than 100 percent because the categories are not mutually exclusive.

As one might expect, the larger the company, the larger the
proportion of expenditures for "in-house" programs. This is
clearly shown in Table 2.4. Among enterprises with more than

TABLE 2.4. Distribution of Expenditures among Major Education-Training Programs, by Company Size

COMPANY SIZE	TUITION AID	OUTSIDE		IN-HOUSE (COMPANY)	TOTAL
		OTHER	TOTAL		
10,000 or more employees	7%	6%	13%	87%	100%
5,000–9,999	16	12	28	72	100
2,500–4,999	26	12	28	72	100
1,000–2,499	33	24	57	43	100
500–999	22	31	53	47	100
All companies	11%	9%	10%	80%	100%

Source: Lusterman, 1977, p. 14.

10,000 employees, only 6 percent of funds are spent on "outside" courses other than those taken under tuition aid, whereas companies with less than 500 employees devote 31 percent of their expenditures to this category. The smaller the company, the more it is forced to rely on external sources and on prepackaged materials to meet its human resource development needs.

Table 2.2 further indicates that in companies of all sizes, executives and senior managers are most likely to receive training through outside seminars and workshops, while supervisors as well as lower ranks are more limited to in-house programs.

Colleges and universities participate directly in employer-sponsored instruction in two ways. They provide a portion of the "outside" courses, and they also constitute a part of "in-house" activity through the delivery of specific programs under contract with the employer. Unfortunately, no aggregate data are available as to the magnitude of either of these contributions. As a result, there is no aggregate information as to the extent to which higher education participates in providing employee development.

It is, of course, known that there are many examples of cooperation between business and higher education. In particular, one can cite a large number of contractual relationships under which colleges or universities provide workshops, seminars, or courses specifically designed for and delivered to the employees of the contracting company. The American Council of Education has just published a *Directory of Joint Ventures* (Fenwick, 1983), which contains many examples of this as well as of other categories of cooperation. The listings indicate a wide range of programs, ranging from brief workshops to entire degree programs, and involving community colleges, four-year institutions as well as comprehensive universities, and public and private institutions. In some cases, such as a contract between Kent State University and Stouffer Foods, the educational institution is asked only to design program content and materials for a supervisory training program to be implemented by corporate trainers. In other cases, the college or university also provides the instruction, such as a program in English language and cultural training for Japanese employees of Procter and Gamble provided by the University of Cincinnati, or a variety of managerial and technical programs contracted by the NCR Corporation from a number of academic institutions.

Most of the examples in the directory are fully funded by the company. But the growing recognition of the economic importance of human resource development, which was discussed in Chapter 1, is reflected in a number of examples of cooperative programs that are partially supported by public economic development funds. In Massachusetts, for example, the Bay State Skills Corporation is a quasi-public body that was created to stimulate cooperation between industry and education in programs aimed at increasing the availability of highly skilled labor. Cited in the ACE directory are contracts between various industries and Southeastern Massachusetts University to retrain unemployed individuals, as well as an arrangement between the Raytheon Corporation and the University of Massachusetts to provide on-site, graduate-level training in various management and technical fields to company employees.

By far the greatest number of examples cited in the ACE directory involve community colleges. The strong orientation of these institutions toward cooperation with business and industry is further illustrated by a recent publication of the American Association of Community and Junior Colleges which describes the Community College Centers for Contracted Programs established at a number of institutions. (Mahoney, 1982; for other information about community college partnerships with business, see Yarrington, 1977; 1980; Bulpitt, 1980). According to this report, approximately thirty-seven community colleges have established special offices responsible for contracting educational services to the private and public sectors in their communities. Fifteen of these are described in detail in the AACJC booklet.

Both the ACE and the AACJC publications illustrate the particular commitment of the two-year institutions to local employment needs and to in-service education. A number of states make a special effort to fill industrial labor needs through their two-year institutions and use this as a major recruiting device in attracting new business. South Carolina, for example, has a statewide system of Technical Education Centers that provide tailor-made programs. (For information, write to the State Board for Technical and Comprehensive Education, 1429 Senate Street, Columbia, S.C. 29201.)

Even for the two-year institutions and even more for the senior institutions, however, most cooperative arrangements involve only a relatively small number of employees. Typically, programs cited in the ACE directory involve less than one hundred students. The community college arrangements vary in size. The State Technical Institute at Memphis reports that in 1981, its Center for Contracted Programs conducted 223 special courses for 70 industries in 53 non-duplicated sites, with a total of 3,303 enrollments. Because some individuals took more than one course, the total number of students served is actually smaller. Mercer County Community College in New Jersey served 2,118 students in 73 contracted programs over a two-year span (Mahoney, 1982). By contrast, many of the other centers cited in the AACJC report enroll only a few hundred students or less in a small number of contracted programs each year. Thus, the aggregate number of employees served by all of these cooperative efforts remains quite small compared to the 12 million course enrollments each year that NCES estimates are employer sponsored. On the whole, then, the prevalent and probably correct impression is that institutions of higher education provide only a small fraction of the totality of employer-sponsored training and education directly.

In addition to the number of programs developed through direct contracts between employers and the educational institutions, there is an indirect relationship. A certain amount of employer-sponsored instruction is provided by college and university faculty who are engaged as consultants on an individual basis, either directly by the firm or by a third-party vendor of training programs. The extent of this faculty involvement is not known. A recent volume of articles discussing sources of faculty income contains tables showing that 9 percent of faculty in doctoral institutions and 14 percent in comprehensive universities and liberal arts colleges indicate "teaching" as their first or second largest source of outside income (Linnell, 1982). These figures encompass all external instruction, including home-institution extension as well as courses in other academic settings. There is no way of inferring what proportion of this "teaching" constitutes employer-sponsored programs. However, as there are several hundred thousand faculty members in higher education, participation of even 1 or 2 percent would represent an appreciable number.

Colleges and universities are further involved in employee development that is paid for by employers through tuition assistance programs. Lusterman (1977) reports that 89 percent of all companies in his survey have arrangements under which employees receive full or partial employer funding for the costs of courses taken at their own initiative and usually on their own time. Plans usually provide for tuition reimbursement after successful completion, sometimes on a sliding scale depending on the grade received. The Conference Board survey indicates that total company expenditures for these plans in 1974–75 amounted to about $25 million. Although this is a substantial amount, it averages out to a very small amount per employee. Almost 60 percent of the surveyed enterprises spent less than $5.00 per employee per year on tuition payments, and only 8 percent reported expenditures of more than $20.00 per employee per year. And the survey again found the pattern, already seen in the distribution of other categories of employer-sponsored instruction, that larger corporations are more involved than smaller ones. Lusterman's results are shown in Table 2.5 in which the *relative* amounts are probably more significant than the absolute numbers.

A more recent survey of 304 corporations provides confirming information (*Recruiting Trends,* 1979). The responding enterprises spent a total of $14.2 million which amounted to an average cost of $245 per *participating* employee and less than $18 as an average for the total work force in the participating companies. Averages per employee ranged from 43 cents to $867, and the average participation rate was reported to be 7 percent of all employees.

T A B L E 2.5. Expenditures per Employee on Tuition Assistance by Percentage of Responding Corporations

$ 0.01 to	$ 2.00	29%
2.01	5.00	29
5.01	10.00	22
10.01	20.00	12
20.01 and over		8

Source: Lusterman, 1977, p. 33.

Tuition aid plans have been extensively studied by the National Institute for Work and Learning, formerly the National Manpower Institute (Wirtz, 1979; Barton, 1982). This work indicates that, nationally, only 3 to 5 percent of all eligible employees and no more than 1 to 2 percent of eligible blue-collar workers make use of these programs. As in all other categories of adult learning, the greater the prior educational attainment, the greater the participation of the individual.

Some corporations and unions that make special efforts to foster educational opportunities for their constituencies have achieved much greater participation rates. Detailed case studies have been carried out, of Kimberley-Clark (Rosow, 1979; see also Barton, 1982), of Polaroid (Knox, 1979; see also Barton, 1982), and of District Council 37 of AFSCME (American Federation of State, County, and Municipal Employees) in New York City (Shore, 1979; see also Barton, 1982). All three are examples of high utilization. The studies indicate the importance of strong employer or union leadership commitment, together with the need for an effective support structure that provides guidance and information to prospective participants. This is also stressed in the *Recruiting Trends* survey mentioned above.

In the cases studied by the NIWL, the supporting services were primarily furnished by the sponsoring employers or unions. However, colleges and universities can do a great deal to stimulate higher participation in tuition assistance plans by taking the initiative in furnishing a variety of advisory services.

In this period of decreasing availability of federal and other sources of financial aid, tuition reimbursement can be of particular importance in offsetting the impact of decreasing availability of federal and other sources of financial aid, and could boost lagging enrollments. A tripling of the current low participation rate in the tuition plans could add another 4 million paid enrollments in higher education (see Gold and Charner, 1983).

In addition to serving academic self-interest in this fashion, more systematic and vigorous involvement by higher education in the development and utilization of tuition assistance plans would constitute a very effective way of improving communication between employers, labor and professional organizations, and educators. Later chapters will emphasize the great need to build better bridges between the academy and the world of work.

Rivaling and probably exceeding these educational institutions as providers is the rapidly growing "training industry." This consists of a large number of proprietary as well as not-for-profit organizations that range in size from one-desk consulting offices to substantial enterprises. One of the largest is the American Management Associations. In 1981, the AMA had more than 100,000 individuals enrolled in management courses and had a tuition income exceeding $40 million (Zemke, 1983, p. 34). The total volume of the training industry is estimated to be more than $1.5 billion annually (Hope, 1983).

Content and Nature

Precise information about the content of employer-sponsored education is as difficult to obtain as data about its cost. However, a number of general characteristics emerge quite clearly from the existing surveys and descriptions. All indicate that by far the greatest portion of the training and development is intended for managers, supervisors, and professionals. Both in number of hours and in cost, this part of the effort is quite disproportionate to the percentage of the entire work force made up by these white-collar workers. Goldstein's (1980) analysis of Lusterman's study indicates that 37 percent of the employees involved and 24 percent of the expenditures reported in the survey were devoted to management/supervisory courses. In addition, 61 percent of the enrollment and 74 percent of the costs were associated with functional/technical courses in areas such as production, maintenance, marketing, sales, office administration, internal systems, and personnel. These are also mostly managerial and white-collar skills. All other categories of programs, including basic skills, constituted only 2 percent of enrollment and costs. These figures contrast sharply with the distribution of occupational groups in the corporate sector, as shown in Table 2.6, taken from the Lusterman study.

The Training Report results (Zemke, 1983, p. 25) are quite consistent with these findings. The following are the five types of content reported most frequently as provided by the companies surveyed:

Supervisory skills	77.1%
New employee orientation	71.2%
Management skills and development	67.3%
Communication skills	58.3%
Technical skills/ knowledge updating	58.2%

It was already mentioned that the report shows that professionals, managers, and supervisors are most likely to receive thirty or more hours of training per year.

The rather lopsided emphasis on relatively advanced instruction is to some extent due to a continuing reliance on apprenticeship and on-the-job training for the lower-wage occupations on the production line and in the office. Systematic, longitudinal studies of the distribution of employer-sponsored education are not available, but there are indications that during the past decade or so it has gradually broadened from a narrow focus primarily on management development to include more and more intermediate and lower employment levels. In recent years, for example, there has been a consider-

TABLE 2.6. Distribution of Occupational Groups in Work Force, by Company Type

Company Type	Managerial	Professional and Technical	Sales and Marketing	Other Non-Exempt	Total
Manufacturing	11%	12%	8%	69%	100%
Transportation, Communications, Utilities	10	10	10	70	100
Wholesale and Retail	9	4	14	73	100
Financial and Insurance	14	14	19	53	100
Other	11	17	5	67	100
All Companies	11%	12%	10%	67%	100%

Source: Lusterman, 1977, p. 16.

able expansion of programs in data and word processing for clerical personnel. This is quite consistent with the changes in the work force discussed in the first chapter, and the view expressed by Drucker (1978) that the replacement of apprenticeship and learning from experience by formal education is gradually spreading to all categories of labor.

To anyone interested in the potential role of colleges and universities in the employer-sponsored system, the most striking fact to emerge from the existing studies is that a substantial portion of the existing programs is at a post-secondary level and that the majority of participants are college graduates. Furthermore, although categories such as new employee orientation and a good deal of technical training are of necessity company- and product-specific, much of corporate education is quite generic. This is clearly indicated by the substantial use of packaged materials and of standardized offerings provided by the training industry. The Training Report estimates expenditures of $680 million for "off-shelf" materials in 1982 (Zemke, 1983, p. 44). Indeed, there is considerable evidence that a good deal of employee development resembles college courses both in content and in format, but nevertheless involves no academic institution in its design or delivery. An indication of this is provided by two systematic and substantial undertakings to evaluate non-collegiate-sponsored instruction and to suggest academic course and credit equivalents. One of these is conducted by the Board of Regents in New York State. Its 1980 *Guide* lists 1,167 courses provided by 107 non-collegiate sources in the state (Regents, 1980). The other is the American Council for Education, which publishes a *National Guide* containing more than 1,000 courses offered by 101 non-educational sources in 25 states (*The National Guide to Non-Collegiate Sponsored Education*, 1982).

A random sampling of these two volumes shows collegelike courses such as "An Introduction to Finance" and "Calculus I and II" offered by General Electric to its employees; "Materials Engineering" and "Modern Structural Analysis" offered by General Motors; "Real Estate Property Management" offered by the Southern California Gas Company; "Accounting," "Corporate Finance," and "Money and Banking" offered by the Manufacturers Hanover Trust Company; and "Multivariate Analysis" and "Statistical Foundations" provided by the New York Telephone Company. In each case, the level and the extent of the course are considered as the equivalent of from one to three college credits.

There is also the much-publicized, but quantitatively less important trend toward formal degree-granting authority by professional associations, proprietary institutions, and corporate units. A recent study (Hawthorne et al., 1983) lists fourteen "corporate colleges" that have degree-granting authority from at least one state and either possess or have applied for non-governmental accreditation. Six among these are or originally were sponsored by a corporation: The General Motors Institute, Northrup University, DeVry Institute (Bell and Howell), Watterson College (Metrodata), Wang Institute, and McDonald's Hamburger University. The oldest, dating back to 1944, is the Institute of Textile Technology, which is a cooperative venture of a number of textile manufacturers. In addition, three consulting firms have degree programs: Arthur D. Little, The American Management Associations, and the Rand Corporation. Further on the list are one hospital (Massachusetts General Hospital) and three trade or professional associations: the Insurance Society of New York, the American Institute of Banking, and the Boston Architectural Center. Another study (Baker, 1983) canvassed several hundred corporations with more than 5,000 employees. Eight companies indicated plans to offer a total of nineteen college-level degree programs during the next five years. These are likely to be in engineering, computer science, and management.

In addition to the full degree programs and many course-length activities, corporations sponsor a very large number of shorter workshops and seminars with material that resembles college offerings. There is, therefore, little doubt that a substantial portion of the corporate "shadow educational system" is similar to undergraduate- or graduate-level instruction. This book addresses itself to the basic question of whether more of this instruction than is presently provided could be supplied by colleges and universities on a contract basis rather than by the corporations themselves or by third-party vendors.

In order to pursue this further, it is useful to explore the purposes rather than just the content of existing programs for employees. Lusterman (1977, p. 5) groups these into three broad categories:

1. Programs to accommodate the growth and turnover in personnel.

2. Programs to meet education and training needs created by changes in the knowledge and skills required by, or available to, a company and its employees.

3. Programs to improve the skills and performance of present employees in their present jobs.

The following discussion will elaborate briefly on each category.

1. The principal need arising from growing numbers of employees and from their natural and inevitable turnover is to prepare individuals for *effective entry into first-level professional, supervisory, and managerial positions*. This entry typically occurs from one of three sources:

- promotion from a so-called non-exempt job into supervisory or professional positions;
- "diagonal" movement from a professional into a supervisory position;
- initial entry, usually after college graduation.

It is understandable that a certain amount of instruction is needed for individuals in the first two of these three groups. They are moving into activities for which, in general, they have not had prior preparation. Since in terms of both demand and content, such instruction is fairly predictable, it is surprising that so few colleges and universities have moved to provide appropriate programs. Only a small number of short courses and workshops exist for newly appointed foremen and supervisors, and there are even fewer college offerings for engineers and other professional personnel who are assuming supervisory and managerial duties. As a result, most of this instruction is provided by the companies either with their own training and development staff or through consultants, proprietary firms, and other vendors.

The current situation with regard to newly hired college graduates raises more serious questions with regard to the role of colleges and universities. It is not the responsibility of these institutions to produce "turnkey" products that are fully prepared to hit the ground running the day they start their first job. A company appropriately provides an initial orientation to its practices and priorities, as well as an introduction to its products. This, obviously, must be provided internally. But one would expect the newly employed college graduates to possess all the necessary basic skills and generic knowledge to function effectively in the corporate context. Unfortunately, this appears not to be the case. To a disconcerting extent, corporate executives are of the opinion that college graduates are improperly and inadequately prepared, even in terms of general background.

Executives in the 610 enterprises surveyed in Lusterman's study were asked to rate educational institutions on their work-preparation role. As shown in Table 2.7, 31 percent of those who mentioned graduate schools rated them as doing a poor job. For undergraduate business schools this percentage rose to 41 percent, and for undergraduate liberal arts colleges to 78 percent. High rates of satisfaction existed only in the area of undergraduate engineering and science, about which only 8 percent of those mentioning these institutions expressed dissatisfaction.

Widespread discontent with professional preparation in colleges and universities has existed in employer circles for a long time. Recently, it has been expressed publicly in many newspaper and magazine articles. The mounting chorus of criticism has been directed at every professional area, including engineering. Chapter 4 will elaborate on this and will discuss in some detail the shortcomings that are widely attributed to pre-professional education.

Because of these perceived inadequacies, companies consider that much of what they have to provide in terms of employee instruction is remedial and should really have been furnished before employment by the educational system. Table 2.8 shows that 27 percent of the executives participating in the Lusterman survey thought that some, much, or all of company pro-

TABLE 2.7. How Executives Rated Educational Institutions on Their Work-Preparation Role

	Believe Institution Performs Work-Preparation Role:		Total Mentions	"Poorly" Percentage of Total Mentions
	Particularly Well	*Particularly Poorly*		
Four-year colleges—engineering/science	44%	4%	48%	8%
Two-year colleges—vocational curriculum	51	7	58	12
Private vocational	29	10	38	25
Graduate schools	28	12	40	31
Four-year colleges—business	28	20	48	41
Secondary schools—vocational curr.	26	27	53	51
Two-year colleges—academic	17	23	40	57
Primary	13	22	34	63
Four-year colleges—liberal arts	10	34	44	78
Secondary—academic curriculum	9	39	48	81

Source: Lusterman, 1977, p. 62.

T A B L E 2.8. Portions of Company Programs that Executives Believe Are "Really the Responsibility of the Schools to Provide"*

Company Size	None	Little	Some	Much	All	Portion Not Indicated	Total
10,000 employees and over	40%	14%	32%	11%	1%	2%	100%
5,000–9,999	49	11	25	8	2	5	100
2,500–4,999	62	9	23	3	—	3	100
1,000–2,499	40	5	26	6	2	1	100
500–999	78	7	11	3	—	1	100
Company Type							
Manufacturing	69	8	18	5	—	—	100
Transportation, Communications, Utilities	50	15	28	4	—	3	100
Wholesale and Retail	71	3	15	2	6	3	100
Financial and Insurance	48	10	30	8	1	3	100
Other	66	4	21	6	—	3	100
Total	63%	8%	21%	5%	1%	2%	100%

*Base is those companies providing any courses for employees during working hours (75 percent of all companies).
Source: Lusterman, 1977, p. 63.

51

T A B L E 2.9.   Percentage of Companies Providing Basic Remedial Education

	AFTER WORK HOURS %	DURING WORK HOURS %	TOTAL DURING AND/OR AFTER %
Company Size			
10,000 employees and over	14	29	35
5,000–9,999	6	14	18
2,500–4,999	12	14	22
1,000–2,499	6	4	10
500–999	*	4	4
Company Type			
Manufacturing	5	7	11
Transportation, communications, utilities	8	8	13
Wholesale, retail	1	2	3
Financial, insurance	6	18	20
Other	6	4	10
All companies	5	8	11

*Less than ¹/₂ of 196.
Source: Lusterman, 1977, p. 64.

grams were "really the responsibility of the schools." Obviously this leads to considerable resentment, just as many faculty members and administrators in higher education resent the need to provide basic skill instruction to make up for deficiencies in high school education. Unfortunately, colleges and universities are, on the whole, not very successful at remedying the limited literacy of their students. It should therefore come as no surprise that corporations are very dissatisfied with the ability of college graduates to communicate effectively. A substantial number of companies provide basic remedial education in communication and numerical skills, as indicated in Table 2.9 taken from the Lusterman study.

A second category of basic skills receives even more attention: with almost complete unanimity, corporate officials feel that college graduates are inadequately or indeed not at all prepared to deal with organizational and interpersonal relationships. Because of this, employer-sponsored education places great emphasis on human interaction and organizational effectiveness in the entry-level orientation and training programs. These typically consist of one or two weeks of intensive instruction. Large companies usually have both the facilities and the staff to provide this themselves repeatedly throughout the year. Small enterprises frequently turn to programs conducted by external providers.

2. A second substantial portion of corporate training is developed *in response to changes in technology, products, organization, or external regulations.* The need for this is obvious, as is the fact that on the whole, this is one area that is not predictable, must be accomplished promptly, and in all probability is non-repetitive.

Instructional activities in this category range widely from short briefing sessions on matters such as compliance with a new federal regulation to elaborate and complex preparations for the launching of a major new product. For months prior to the distribution of a new category of computers, a company will be preparing a whole curriculum of training materials for its sales force, service personnel, and others who will have to be familiar with the new product. A growing amount of this material is being produced in the form of video cassettes, computerized instruction, satellite-transmitted teleconferences, and other methods that allow the necessary training to take place in many locations and at flexible times. At the same time, traditional printed manuals continue to be used extensively.

Also falling into this category of employer-sponsored instruction is the preparation given to individuals who are slated for overseas assignments. This preparation consists primarily of intensive language training, provided by one of the several commercial firms specializing in this, and is at times supplemented by brief workshops—in some cases including the employee's family—on cross-cultural issues. Here again, the relative lack of involvement by language and foreign-area specialists at our colleges and universities is surprising, and indicates a lack of adaptability to employers' needs for very different instructional formats and locations.

3. The two categories of employer-sponsored instruction discussed above exist to some extent throughout the entire corporate sector. In addition, many companies also support a substantial *continuing education and training effort for professionals and managers.* Some of this is intended to provide individuals with opportunities for improving their work-related competence and skills and to keep them up to date with regard to policies and procedures of the company, external issues, and the like. Most of the emphasis, however, appears to be on providing appropriate instruction in connection with continuing upward movement across the several significant hierarchical bridge points. The larger the company, the more explicit is the distinction between programs for first-line managers, middle managers, advanced managers, and executives.

The variety of lectures, seminars, workshops, and courses existing throughout the corporate sector is so great that they defy simple categorization. Lusterman (1977, pp. 86–90) describes a sampling of these various types of offerings. Most of the offerings appear to be related to management or administration, with typical titles such as "Marketing Concepts and Strategies," "Financial Management and Control," "The Computer as a Management Tool," and "Negotiating Skills." Especially in technologically oriented industries, there are also many scientific and technical courses, including "Catalysis Science," "Instrumentation and Process Control," "Solid-State Electronics," and many others. In addition, a small number of offerings deal with contextual issues, such as "Business-Government Relations," as well as lectures on current events.

These course titles, again, indicate a good deal of similarity between employer-sponsored courses and the usual components of higher-education curricula. The courses vary as widely in length as they do in content. Most are short, ranging from a few hours to a few days in duration. Some extend over several weeks or even months, usually scheduled for one or two late afternoons or evenings a week. Most of the in-house activities occur at the work site, but a few of the larger corporations supplement these with courses offered at one or more centralized locations. In some cases, the locations are elaborate and attractive campuses that look like many colleges or universities, and are complete with residential and recreational facilities. These sites host a steady succession of employee groups for periods ranging from one to several weeks.

The more advanced the employee's level, the more use is made of existing advanced management and executive training programs conducted on campuses by many business schools and other academic units throughout the country. These range from short courses to thirteen-week sessions, and there are directories listing and describing them for the benefit of divisional managers and human resource directors who are responsible for assigning personnel to such courses (see Bricker, 1981; McNulty, 1980; AMA, 1978). Some companies publish their own list of preferred programs for internal use.

In addition to appropriate programs in colleges and universities, and workshops and seminars organized by a wide variety of consulting firms and professional associations, limited use is also made of tuition remission plans and, in some cases, of company-supported leaves for full-time graduate study.

The great majority of employer-sponsored continuing education is conceived in terms of distinct units that are designed to be free standing and are not viewed as part of an overall pattern. Larger enterprises may have entry programs that usually last one to three years and combine on-the-job training with some periods of formal instruction. For employees who are already in supervisory or managerial capacities, some large corporations have elaborate, multiyear schemes in which managers on their way up alternate at regular intervals between in-house and external programs. In most cases, individuals are identified for these successive stages of development at some time while they are at the preceding managerial level. Some of the largest companies, however, have in recent years instituted more of a long-range developmental approach in order to ensure the availability of proper candidates for top executive positions in ten or twenty years' time. In such a "successor-planning system," strategic planning includes estimates of future needs at senior executive levels. This leads to the identification, at a very early stage of their career in the company, of about three times the ultimately needed number of highly promising young managers. These individuals follow a sophisticated and elaborate "fast track" plan for development, which combines successive periods of training and education, as described before, with a series of appointments in different segments of the corporation (Shaeffer, 1972).

One of the most elaborate programs of executive development ment exists at IBM (Moulton, 1981). Selected middle-management and executive personnel attend an alternating sequence of in-house and external programs. These are scheduled throughout the individual's career at three- to five-year intervals. The sequence includes three internal activities focused on IBM:

- a three-week "Advanced Management School" designed for high-potential middle managers, with a curriculum concentrating on the company, the managerial process, and the business environment;
- a one-week "Executive Seminar" for executives, which covers IBM's strategic issues as well as external economic, social, and political developments;
- a two-week "International Executive Program" which brings together senior IBM executives from all parts of the multinational enterprise and concetrates on strategic international issues facing IBM.

All three of these programs are conducted by top IBM executives together with outside speakers for groups of about twenty.

These internal activities alternate with external ones that fall into four categories:

- "General Management" programs, usually offered by graduate business schools at major universities such as Harvard, MIT, Pennsylvania, or Stanford;
- "Leadership" programs, concentrating on interpersonal effectiveness at the executive level, at a variety of institu-

tions including non-academic ones like the Menninger Institute;
- "Public Affairs" programs, dealing with federal operations and national policy issues, and often provided in Washington by the Brookings Institute or the American Enterprise Institute;
- "Humanities" programs focusing on man, society, and values. The best known example of this is the Executive Seminar of the Aspen Institute.

The IBM executive development strategy is described here in some detail because it illustrates both the strengths and the weaknesses of one of the best programs of its kind. On the one hand, it indicates considerable thought and represents, in its aggregate, a substantial investment by the corporation. In addition, it provides for the individual managers and executives a variety of important benefits well beyond the content of the various courses. Their participation earns them the label of "comers" and allows them to meet their counterparts in other divisions of the company and often other people who are much higher up in the hierarchy, in an informal yet intensive setting that often leads to lasting relationships. Last but not least, it provides them with a refreshing intellectual change of pace at regular intervals.

On the other hand, when one remembers that the succession of these activities extends over a period of twenty years or more, it does not represent a large amount of time spent in formal education. If each external program takes an average of two weeks, the total adds up to about fifteen weeks spread over two decades, equivalent to between 1 and 2 percent of the total time of the participating employees. Weinstein (1982) estimates that the total cost of employer-sponsored education is about twice the value of the time spent by the participants. However, only a limited portion of the staff participates in instructional programs in any one year. Combining these factors, one arrives at a very inexact guess that IBM may spend the equivalent of about 1 percent of its payroll on organized employee education each year. Of course, this 1 percent represents a very appreciable amount, especially in a corporation such as IBM. Employees also acquire new knowledge in a wide variety of informal ways that cannot be quantified for inclusion in this estimate. Yet, it is not much of an investment in human resource development and maintenance, especially as compared with the more than 10 percent of operating costs that IBM devotes to research, development, and engineering, and the approximately 7 percent spent for plant, equipment, and other physical property (IBM, 1983).

CHAPTER 3

The Role of Colleges and Universities

THE FOREGOING BROAD-BRUSH DESCRIPTION of existing employer-sponsored training and education programs shows that a substantial portion of such training is generic, at a level corresponding to undergraduate instruction, and with subject matter that could be offered by academic institutions. Yet it is also clear that at this time the role played by colleges and universities in the "shadow system" is quite limited.

It is therefore important to examine first whether increased participation of academic institutions is desirable. If this appears to be the case, one can then proceed to identify the barriers to such collaboration.

The issue is not whether colleges and universities should assume *sole* or even *primary* responsibility for employee education. As the development and maintenance of human capital become more important, the responsibility for this task inevitably becomes more and more disaggregated. No one system and no single set of institutions can or should retain a monopoly of education and training. There are highly legitimate and important roles for in-house human resource development as well as for a vigorous training industry. For one thing, there is the

59

issue of scale: all of the advanced management and executive training programs currently existing in colleges and universities in this country could not handle the combined needs of the corporate sector. In addition, the location of many companies is not convenient to the principal concentrations of educational institutions. Modern educational technology may reduce the problems both of scale and of location, but under no circumstance can one envision a situation in which business and industry rely entirely on academic institutions. At this time, however, they use them only to a very limited extent, and the question worth addressing is whether this reliance should and can be greater.

The considerable amount of money spent by the private sector on employee education is, of course, itself a strong incentive for colleges and universities that are facing shrinking enrollments of traditional college-age students, decreasing state and federal support, and dire economic prospects. But should academic institutions pursue these corporate funds? Would they be selling their intellectual birthright for a mess of pottage? Would this be an example of the danger to academic integrity that arises when, in the words of Boyer and Hechinger (1981, p. 58), "campuses turn themselves into educational supermarkets with a view toward mere fiscal survival"?

The danger indeed exists if academic institutions become more involved in corporate education solely for financial reasons. But although that is an important motivation, it is not the principal justification for moving in that direction. Higher education must intensify its obligation to concern itself with society's human capital and manpower needs. It has an inescapable responsibility, again to quote Boyer and Hechinger, "to transmit knowledge that would be useful, not merely in the classical sense of preparing gentlemen, but for the practical demands of a changing world" (p. 9).

By and large, this has been the guiding principle of American higher education from its very inception. Harvard's education was initially designed, in large measure, as training for the ministry. Its classical curriculum was well suited for this purpose, and even when not used as professional preparation, it had an eminently practical purpose. Oscar and Mary Handlin, in their book on the American college (Handlin and Handlin, 1970), observe that John Adams went to Harvard because its "course of learning endowed those who completed it with the cultural attributes that were signs of superior status" (p. 10). What could be more career oriented than that?

Veysey, in *The Emergence of the American University* (1965), and Brubacher and Rudy, in *Higher Education in Transition* (1968), provide excellent descriptions of the ongoing debate in the development of higher education in this country between emphases on utility and on liberal culture. On the whole, the arguments increasingly revolved around what would be the best mix of these two elements to prepare young people for their future. What should be the balance between liberal breadth and vocational specialization, between theory and practice? Although well into the twentieth century, some argued that the cultivation of the mind was the sole purpose of higher education, this essentially aristocratic conception was rejected by the majority inside the academy and almost everyone outside. Brubacher and Rudy point out that

the social equalitarianism of democracy had filed down the sharp distinction between those who worked and those who did not. Indeed in twentieth century democracy nearly everyone worked. Where work was well nigh universal it would be difficult to maintain the traditional division between liberal and illiberal subjects. [1968, p. 303]

This is entirely consistent with the statement quoted earlier that a person's capacities for practical activity cannot be meaningfully decomposed into vocational and liberal components.

A few pages later in their study, Brubacher and Rudy state that in the debate about the goals and purposes of higher education, the public's voice had constituted "a rising crescendo in favor of a higher education amenable to their changing needs" (1968, p. 306). In short, for at least the past century there was never any serious question that colleges and universities should prepare young people for effective participation in the world of work as well as in the democratic process. The disagreement was about means, not ends, and focused on how much specialization was required to provide such preparation.

In *Academic Revolution,* the extraordinary account of the growth and transformation of American higher education after World War II, Jencks and Riesman (1968) state quite bluntly that there was never any serious question about the role of higher education in career preparation. They dismiss the frequent complaint that "the nation's colleges have been corrupted by vocationalism," and that "in the good old days . . . colleges were pure and undefiled seats of learning [where] students came to get a liberal education." This, they point out, is a myth, and:

> Like other pastoral idylls, this myth serves all sorts of polemical purposes, good and bad. But it is a myth nevertheless. . . . Young men of college age worried about their future careers in the colonial era just as they do today, and this affected both the kind of men who came to college and the kinds of things they did once they arrived. During the colonial era people usually went to college because they hoped to become clergymen; today they go because they hope to become doctors, lawyers, business executives and the like. [p. 199]

With the development of professional schools and the passage of the Land Grant Act of 1862, the purpose of higher education as a preparation for a career became more explicit. Education expanded to provide skills for increasingly sophisticated occupations in the growing manufacturing industries. Both enrollment patterns and curricula were determined increasingly by manpower needs and market considerations.

One might have expected this trend to accelerate after the Second World War, when this country quite consciously moved toward mass higher education as a matter of public policy. Indeed, the creation and rapid growth of the community-college sector was characterized by strong ties to the work place and continuing adjustment to changing manpower demands.

In one fundamental sense, this also happened with the college and university sector. Its expansion was accompanied by the trend discussed in Chapter 1. Educational requirements of almost all occupations increased across sectors of the economy. A college degree became the prerequisite for a growing list of jobs. And not just any college degree. Growing educational expectations were accompanied by increased professionalization. More and more occupations were open only to individuals with specialized training. In some European countries this led to the creation of large numbers of separate schools, colleges, and institutes that have no ties to the traditional university. In this country, however, almost all advanced specialization became a university monopoly, following a trend set in earlier decades in medicine, law, and agriculture. As a result, the principal enrollment growth occurred in the widening array of professional schools in the American comprehensive university with a corresponding decrease in the *proportion* (not the absolute number) of students majoring in the liberal arts (Jencks and Riesman, 1968, p. 200). Thus, in one sense, the growth of the university sector was accompanied, as well, by shifts in the enrollment patterns and the proliferation of new areas of specialization.

Universities also changed in another way. In *The Uses of the University,* Clark Kerr (1963) describes the new "multi-versity" as having "no peers in all history among institutions of higher learning in serving so many of the segments of advancing civilization" (p. 45). More recently, President Bok of Harvard University has written a very thoughtful book about the social responsibilities of modern universities, entitled *Beyond the Ivory Tower.* In it, he states that "as society came to rely more and more on universities, universities in turn grew ever more dependent on society for money required to support their expanding activities. After World War II, therefore, the image of the ivory tower grew obsolete" (Bok, 1982, p. 7).

Most of the larger universities, particularly those in the public sector, now contain a number of components and activities for various kinds of outreach, technical assistance, and public service. But these new elements have for the most part remained peripheral to the enterprise, ignored, or even denigrated by most of the faculty. Basic research and instruction for full-time, younger students have remained the core of the institutions. For the vast majority of colleges and universities this core continues to be patterned on the model of the traditional research university. And, in turn, this category of institutions has changed very little during the post-war decades. In a postscript to a new edition of *The Uses of the University*, Kerr (1982) writes that "the American research university remains pretty much the same. . . . [It is] among the least changed of institutions."

Thus, during a period of profound societal changes and of major growth in higher education, most of the new or expanded institutions used a role model that has remained substantially unchanged. University education went through a fundamental evolution from being for the few and the young to being for the many and all ages. But this happened without systematic exploration of whether these changes require modifications of the procedures, priorities, and value system of the academic enterprise (Lynton, 1983c).

And we now face the consequences of a substantial and disturbing paradox. The university sector has expanded in response to *external* needs: the baby boom and the growing societal demand for skilled professionals in an expanding number of fields. But the essential center of the university continues to be driven by *internal* values and priorities that have changed little or not at all from those that prevailed before the war under quite different circumstances.

The failure to examine the basic assumptions and modes of university growth was largely due to two factors. First, the expansion of higher education was accompanied in most countries by substantial increases in support for basic and applied research, particularly in the sciences and engineering and in health-related fields. A close look is likely to show, not surprisingly, that a large proportion of these research funds went to a relatively small number of institutions—to a great extent, in fact, those that had existed and had a strong research component before the large expansion. Yet, that pot of gold was there, and all universities scrambled for it. Success in capturing research grants became a major measure—indeed perhaps the principal measure—of institutional quality.

The second major factor that tended to make the new universities into clones of the old ones was that the academy viewed itself as its own principal labor market. The rapid growth created a very large demand for new faculty. Doctoral programs blossomed everywhere to meet this need as well as the needs of the expanding non-university research and development complex. Consequently, not only graduate but also undergraduate education became forced into the singular mold of being a preparation for academic and quasi-academic careers. The discipline became dominant. The most pernicious impact was on the arts and sciences, which lost their "liberal" character. Undergraduate curricula were tailored to prepare for a career in basic research, and faculties focused their energies and pedagogic interests on reproducing themselves.

In the universities and even in the most prestigious four-year institutions, the central undergraduate unit became what Jencks and Riesman (1968) describe as the "university college," a term they attribute to Frank Bowles. A university college is "a college whose primary purpose is to prepare students for graduate study of some kind—primarily in the arts and sciences but also in professional subjects ranging from law and medicine to business and social work" (p. 20).

The most highly regarded "university colleges" are "de facto prep school[s]" for just a few graduate and professional schools. They draw most of their students from the top tenth of the national ability distribution and send a substantial proportion of them to graduate school. If they are part of a university, they have the same faculty as the graduate school of arts and sciences. If separate, they nevertheless "draw . . . [their] faculty from the same manpower pool as the graduate schools of arts and sciences, seeking the same virtues and looking askance at the same presumed vices" (Jencks and Riesman, 1968, p. 24).

Probably only a small proportion of the more than 2,000 undergraduate colleges in this country really fit the full description given by Jencks and Riesman of the "university college." But this description provides the model that many of the other undergraduate colleges regard as desirable. As a result, the arts and sciences have tended to lose ther liberal character and to become academic professions. Throughout higher education the prestige ladder for teaching became one in which "the greatest prestige is associated with teaching those who will follow the subject professionally" (Hughes, 1973, p. 289).

There was a similar impact on the professional schools. As stated earlier, in this country specialized and professional education at the post-secondary level became, with few exceptions, the task of colleges and universities. Back in 1918, already, Thorsten Veblen at Chicago warned against this. He had a very exclusive view of intellectual pursuits, and predicted that the inclusion of the "technicians" of the professional schools in a university:

> unavoidably leads them to court a specious appearance of scholarship and so to invest their technological discipline with a degree of pedantry and sophistication; whereby it is hoped to give these schools and their work some scientific and scholarly prestige. [Veblen, 1918, p. 23]

Veblen, of course, represents the extreme traditionalist view so well described by Bok as seeming to call:

> for a more cloistered institution paying little attention to the immediate problems of society. The specialized training and expert advice that the nation requires would presumably be left to other institutions— vocational schools, consulting firms, institutes of applied research, and think tanks of various kinds. [Bok, 1982, p. 7]

Veblen was concerned lest the presence of professional schools taint the pristine purity of the academy. In fact, the opposite happened: professional schools increasingly became assimilated into what Parsons and Platt (1973) describe so well as the "core of cognitive primacy" of the university. The schools patterned themselves after the most prestigious element of the university: the arts and sciences. They shifted their focus from a concern with the profession to an interest in its disciplinary components. They increasingly became graduate schools in these disciplines, oriented more toward their own development than to the needs of the profession, resulting in an increasing divergence between professional preparation and professional practice.

As curricular emphasis in both the arts and sciences and the professional fields became increasingly theoretical and abstract, university education moved ever further away from what Alfred North Whitehead thought it should be: "the acquisition of the art of the utilization of knowledge" (Whitehead, 1929, p. 6). *The focus of higher education is now almost entirely on the acquisition of knowledge and no longer on the competence to use it.*

This is reflected as well in the faculty reward system which is determined almost exclusively by the internal values and priorities of the academic community. Emphasis is placed only on a single mode of scholarly activity: basic research leading to publication in scholarly journals directed at colleagues in the profession. More applied work and other forms of disseminating knowledge, such as technical assistance and direct interaction with private- and public-sector users, have become downgraded. In addition, many faculty, particularly in the social sciences, believe that practical problem solving and policy making can be reduced to a scientific activity susceptible to their disciplinary methodology. The fallacy in this was recently pointed out by Lindblom and Cohen (1979).

This attitude both contributed to and was intensified by the changing nature of the faculty in higher education as it expanded to keep pace with institutional growth. Most of the new recruits to academic ranks were themselves a product of the post-war universities. They went through a narrowly specialized undergraduate curriculum that had been designed as preparation for graduate work and research, they proceeded into the latter, and then without interruption assumed academic positions. As a result, the new faculty in many cases were not broadly educated and not particularly interested in fields other

than their own. Furthermore, they knew little of related professional activities and applied work outside of the academy and
were less and less able to help their students in the transition
from the classroom to any job outside academia.

All of this has created a considerable divergence between
higher education and the rest of society. Consequently, there
now exists a real question about the future role of higher education in meeting the country's growing need for a labor force
that enters employment with real competence and maintains
effectiveness through lifelong education.

It is the basic premise of this book that the purposes of
higher education should again become related to external
needs. This premise is based on several reasons. Some clearly
reflect the self-interest of academic institutions. Colleges and
universities are facing decreasing enrollments in the traditional
age range. Moreover, they find themselves in growing competition with other social agencies and human services for a shrinking pool of public resources. These conditions constitute strong
motives for higher education institutions to increase their role
in providing employer-sponsored instruction.

But there are other reasons for more participation that are
less self-serving and that suggest that greater involvement by
colleges and universities can be important and beneficial to employers and to society generally, as well as to the academic institutions.

In the first place, it might be more cost-effective for employers to "buy" rather than to "make"—the traditional choice that
pertains to many of the supporting services needed by an enterprise. All current surveys indicate that at this time business
and industries "make" a lot of courses that are very similar to
academic products. Much of the instruction organized in-house
and taught by corporate staff or by paid consultants is generic
and equivalent to college courses. It might be more advantageous for employers to "buy" these products *if they were readily
available* when, where, and in the format most convenient to the
client, and with an approach to content that is pertinent to their
needs. The next chapter will discuss the fact that unfortunately
this is usually not the case. Colleges and universities are gener-

ally inflexible and unresponsive, and tend to be too abstract and too theoretical. As a result, the corporate sector has tended to follow the path of least resistance and developed its own educational system instead of putting more pressure on academic institutions to accommodate its needs. This emphasis on "making" rather than "buying" may well be leading to extra costs and wasteful duplication. A senior official of General Motors, responsible for providing management training and consulting services worldwide to all parts of the corporate organizations and its affiliated dealers and distributors, has recently been quoted as saying:

> Major industries maintain very large staffs of their own to meet their continuing education needs, but they do so principally because they can't find viable providers through academic sources. We simply would not hire people and maintain them on the payroll if there were an alternative, but so far we haven't seen an alternative. The point is simply this: There are very few unique things internal to a company of a continuing education nature; these things could be done just as effectively—or more effectively—if the academic community would take the initiative to go after that kind of business. But we don't see that happening, even though we'd rather buy than make. [Kost, 1980, p. 51]

The premise of the book is based on a further rationale for adaptations in higher education—a rationale that transcends economic considerations. Increased participation of colleges and universities in employer-sponsored instruction would be a highly effective way of reducing academic isolation and of making faculties as well as administrators more aware of and more sensitive to the practical needs and conditions of the work place. In turn, this can have a substantial impact on the quality and effectiveness of undergraduate and graduate education in both professional schools and the liberal arts units. It can result in a significant improvement in the competence and effectiveness of those who graduate from academic institutions. That would clearly benefit employers and reduce the need for costly investment in the kind of remediation and filling of gaps discussed in Chapter 2. More important, it would enhance the contribution of higher education to the formation as well as the maintenance of that human capital which is so necessary to the economic and social vitality of out post-industrial society.

And yet another reason must be added. In spite of all the criticism that can be leveled against higher education, it constitutes an enormously important asset to our society. It is the best—indeed perhaps the only—way to assure an appropriate balance of long-range considerations with short-term responses and to combine liberal breadth with narrowly oriented skills. It is the only mechanism that can combine the necessary degree of detachment with responsiveness to immediate pressures, and is the best guarantee of quality in the ever more important process of human resource development.

Thus, the corporate sector and society in general would be better served by insisting on the necessary adaptations in the system of higher education that would make it serve its human capital needs, rather than by continuing to expand its own alternatives. A greater role in employee education for colleges and universities will benefit all participants and is not merely a matter of academic self-interest.

But for this to happen, the academy must face up to the need for a number of profound changes in its procedures and methodologies, in its pedagogic approaches, and in its relationships to the non-academic world.

CHAPTER 4

The Need for Change in the Academy

Procedural Changes

Institutions, like individuals, are creatures of habit. Often these habits have little intrinsic value, except convenience within a given context. For example, knowledge does not by nature come in packages of three lectures a week delivered for fourteen weeks, but most colleges and universities over the years have found this format to be convenient as well as pedagogically feasible for a full-time, resident student body. It would seem to be a simple matter to adapt this format to different needs of different clienteles, but it is dangerous to underestimate either institutional or individual resistance to changing the "way things have always been done."

Yet such procedural changes are among the most important ones to be made if colleges and universities are indeed to take a more active role in the provision of employer-sponsored education. The instructional needs of the corporate world are manifold, their timing and predictability variable, and their optimal location usually not on campus. Some corporate educational needs arise unexpectedly. Others could be predicted with reasonable lead time but are often not recognized or at least not acted on until the last moment. A later chapter will address the great need for more systematic planning and anticipation on the part of the employer. But even under the most ideal circumstances, corporate sponsors will expect from the colleges and universities a far shorter response time to their needs than is now possible under the usual academic program review and approval procedures. If academic institutions are to provide a larger fraction of that broad array of corporate education, they must develop a degree of flexibility as well as a speed of response that would constitute a sharp departure from current practices and procedures.

It is true that a growing number of colleges and universities have been quite aggressive in expanding their continuing and adult education programs. Many can deliver a great variety of offerings quickly and in a wide range of non-traditional formats. But on the whole, these forms of instruction are organized and administered outside of the core structure of the institution. The activities are peripheral and receive at best limited faculty involvement and oversight. Changing this situation is probably the most important as well as the most difficult of the adaptations required if colleges and universities are to play a more important role in employer-sponsored instruction.

In the long run it is not satisfactory to continue to deal with this issue by bypassing academic review altogether, as is usually the case for continuing education and extension programs. Although this does enhance institutional responsiveness, it tends to throw out too many babies with the bath water. The principle of academic oversight and faculty involvement is too important. A way must be found to retain these important features but to reduce the length and complexity of the usual review process. At issue is not only the question of faculty control over academic issues. The best way of ensuring that the faculty—and the administration—take non-traditional teaching, such as employer-sponsored education, seriously is to maintain academic oversight. Only if the faculty is directly involved will it accept these activities as constituting as much a part of the central responsibility of the institution as the more traditional instruction of full-time graduate and undergraduate students.

The basic issue in this transcends procedure and organization. We have entered an age in which individuals of all ages require, or at least desire, the kinds of courses and programs that used to be largely confined to a lower age group. What we think of as undergraduate or graduate education is no longer a commodity dispensed only to young people preparing for a career. It is now in demand by a much broader spectrum of the population. Colleges and universities, therefore, must face up to a very clear and immensely important choice: are they institutions defined by *what* they teach, regardless of the nature of the student body, or are they to be characterized by *whom* they teach?

Currently the bulk of continuing and adult education is carried out by institutional elements that are peripheral and have relatively low standing. This suggests that most of our colleges and universities appear to define themselves in terms of the latter criterion. They act as if they were primarily institutions to teach the young. That self-definition is dangerous for the academy, and in the long run, probably also detrimental to society. It would leave the principal responsibility for instruction of the older population to non-academic sources. That is bad for colleges and universities not only because it excludes them from a large portion of the educational market, but also because it enhances their intellectual isolation just when growing communication and interaction are becoming increasingly important. But it also is likely to deprive society at large from making the most effective use of its educational systems.

Instead, colleges, and particularly universities, should define themselves in terms of *what* they teach, and then adapt their procedures and policies so that they may serve all potential clienteles for this instruction. In particular, they should assume primary responsibility for professional education, and accept a much broader definition of the term. This primary responsibility should include both the initial preparation to *become* effective, and subsequently the provision of what is needed to *maintain* the necessary skills and competences. The aggregate of needs in preparation and maintenance far exceeds the capacity of the existing colleges and universities. As has been stated more than once in earlier chapters, substantial portions of the total demand must be provided by corporate in-house programs, by the training industry, and by a variety of other sources of knowledge and information. But institutions of higher education, for the sake of their own survival as well as in order to enhance the overall quality of the collective enterprise, must play an important role. This will require institutional modifications that involve the core of the enterprise and not just some peripheral organizational unit. It requires an appropriate change not only in the operation of the institution, but in its self-image and attitude. The university must learn to recognize *all* of its teaching—credit and non-credit, young and old, full-time and part-time, on and off campus—as equally important and equally central parts of a coherent whole, the quality of which is the collective responsibility of the faculty.

This will require a number of important changes in the organization and the operation of most universities and senior colleges. Paramount among these is the need to wipe out the dividing line between "regular" and "continuing" education. The two terms, and their equivalents, describe a distinction without a difference, even without considering employer-sponsored education. Throughout the country, the average age of college students is steadily increasing. The proportion of students over thirty years of age enrolled in higher education increased from less than 10 percent in 1970 to 22 percent in 1980, and is likely to increase further to about 30 percent in 1990. The enrollment of students twenty-five years or older increased by 88 percent from 2.4 to 4.5 million in the decade between 1970 and 1980, and already constitutes almost 40 percent of the total. In another ten years almost half of all students in colleges and universities are likely to be twenty-five or older. The change in the age profile of enrollment in higher education is strikingly represented in Figure 4.1, reproduced from the NCES report containing the data quoted above (Frankel and Gerald, 1982).

The trend in age distribution has been accompanied by a similar change from full-time to part-time attendance. The proportion of the latter increased from 32 percent in 1970 to

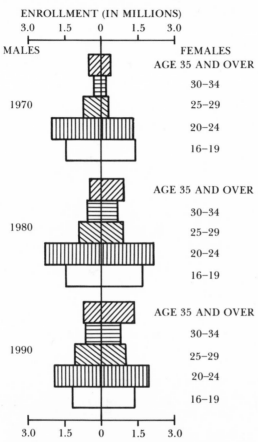

FIGURE 4.1. Total enrollment in all institutions of higher education, by age and sex: 50 States and D.C., 1970, 1980 and 1990. *Source:* Frankel and Gerald, 1982, p. 11.

41 percent in 1980 and is likely to grow further to about 50 percent by 1990. This is shown in Figure 4.2. At the same time, although no aggregate data appear to be available, there is a growing prevalence of interrupted study with intervals of "stopping out."

When the preponderant pattern of enrollment was that of students between eighteen and twenty-four years who enrolled on a full-time basis immediately after high school and con-

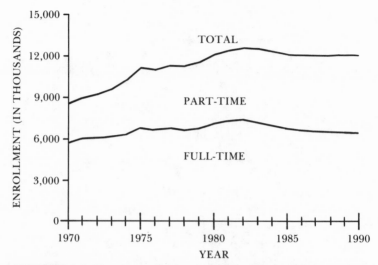

FIGURE 4.2. Total enrollment in institutions of higher education, with intermediate alternative projections, by attendance
status: 50 States and D.C., fall 1970 to 1990. *Source:* Frankel
and Gerald, 1982, p. 28.

tinued without significant interruption until a first or second
degree, it made sense to view "continuing education" as a distinct component of college and university activities. However,
that pattern now constitutes at most one-half of current enrollment, and there is no longer much sense in trying to draw a
dividing line between "regular" and "continuing" education in
the area of credit-bearing instruction.

Similarly, albeit at a slower pace, many of the distinctions
between credit and non-credit instruction provided by academic institutions have become less meaningful. The need to accommodate an ever more heterogeneous student body with ir-
regular patterns of attendance is forcing much credit instruction to be "packaged" into short, intensive periods such as
weekend colleges and total-immersion language instruction.
More and more institutions are providing or sponsoring
televised programs for both credit and non-credit purposes,
the difference usually consisting of studying some subsidiary

material and writing a paper or taking an examination in order to obtain credit.

In short, colleges and universities are now engaged in a spectrum of didactic activities whose extremes fall into the traditional categories of "regular" and "continuing" education, but are now connected by a continuum containing all possible intermediate modes. Maintaining the traditional categories is no longer realistic. It is, in fact, dysfunctional and constitutes a substantial barrier to bringing about necessary adaptations in higher education. Whenever we make a distinction, we also tend to set up a hierarchy of values and status. As long as "continuing education" is viewed as a distinct activity, it will be viewed as outside the mainstream and less important, less respectable, and less central than "regular education."

Wiping out this outdated distinction and recognizing that "continuing education" has become a central part of the mission of higher education changes the role as well as the organizational locus of the traditional Office or Division of Continuing Education. The time is overdue to make it an integral part of the central academic administration of each institution. For many years, the pattern in most colleges and universities has been to keep the continuing education units at arm's length. They were viewed, as was stated recently by one of the foremost leaders in the field, "as peripheral, as frills, a marginal activity to be tolerated or at best as a 'service' subordinate to 'teaching' and 'research'" (Stern, 1980, p. 3).

Elsewhere, Stern states that:

> universities . . . have regarded continuing education as adjunct to their basic purpose. Even in land grant universities the last thirty years have seen an erosion of the sense of higher purpose represented by the phrase "public service." And even public universities continue to slight continuing education and to ignore the competitive threat from outside the campus. [p. 9]

Continuing education must move to a central and highly visible organizational location, similar in universities to research or to graduate education, through a vice presidency or senior position in the office of the chief academic official.

At the same time, if continuing education, like research and graduate education, is to be accepted and developed as an integral part of the institutional purpose, it must also become integrated with the institutional activities. If indeed there is to be an administrative as well as a conceptual continuum linking all forms of instruction into a coherent whole, then continuing education must become an inseparable portion of the instructional responsibilities of the core faculty.

This requires, in the first place, that the role of Offices or Divisions of Continuing Education change from being separate instructional resources to becoming coordinating and facilitating mechanisms. Just as the institutional offices involved in research and graduate work are essentially catalysts to stimulate and to support the activities of the faculty in these areas, the institutional office for continuing education should become the principal change agent to enhance faculty and institutional activity in that part of the continuous spectrum of instruction. Understandably, this is not a universally held view. A number of individuals deeply dedicated to the outreach responsibilities of higher education fear that forcing continuing education into an academic mold and into the traditional organizational governance structures will so shackle it as to make it ineffective. These arguments are described in an excellent discussion of the organization of continuing education by Gordon (1980), who also states the countervailing view that if this activity remained substantially separate from the university, the inevitable result would be "the status of a wholly disowned subsidiary."

In essence, the office of continuing education—whatever its official name—should become the principal boundary-spanning mechanism needed to relate the university to clienteles other than the traditional high school graduate. At this time, the core of the typical college or university has only one such bridging mechanism that links it to the traditional student cohort. It is the complex of recruiting, admissions, and financial offices that, together with registrar and bursar, provide the necessary bridge for a two-way flow of communication that informs the external clientele about the institution and sensitizes the latter to the changing nature and needs of the former. The same bridge in communication is very much needed for the expanding range of non-traditional students, and each institution needs to consider how best to accomplish this. The traditional high-school-oriented offices visit secondary institutions, maintain relationships with guidance counselors and are sensitive to the evolving needs and interests of high school graduates. Similarly, the expertise and the contacts of the continuing education office can provide the essential relationship between the world of work and the academic institution and help to adapt the procedures and policies of the latter to the needs of the former.

One of the key issues in this adaptation revolves around the question of whether institutional outreach to participate in employer-sponsored education should be organized in a centralized or in a decentralized fashion. This is extensively discussed in Gordon's article (1980). There are some clear advantages to decentralization, with various divisions and schools each taking responsibility for the development and delivery of its own programs. There is more direct and immediate faculty involvement, and this can lead to the rapid development of what Gordon describes as "mutually supportive identifications" between the programs and the units that assume responsibility for them. Decentralization also enables some enterprising schools and colleges to move well ahead of a lagging institutional commitment. However, the arguments for centralization are sufficiently cogent to suggest the need for at least a degree of central coordination and oversight. Decentralized operations are likely to be more costly in the aggregate, duplicate efforts, and confusing to many potential clients who require the services of more than one unit. But beyond these functional arguments, there are two overriding reasons for at least partial centralization. First, again in close analogy to research and graduate work, it is useful to have one central locus to stimulate activities and to sensitize all participants to their special needs, circumstances, and opportunities. Second, as stated repeatedly in this book, there is a growing need, particularly in employer-sponsored education, for a breadth that cuts across the boundaries of any one collegiate unit.

One of the principal fears of those who would like to retain autonomy for continuing education is that placing it into an "academic mold" will rob it of all flexibility and responsiveness. Every program would be subject to cumbersome and time-consuming review and approval procedures and any mode of delivery other than three weekly lectures on campus would be viewed with suspicion. There is much justification for this fear, and indeed the prevalence of these habits constitutes one of the principal reasons why employers do not use colleges and universities more than they do. It is absolutely essential to bring about substantial change without sacrificing the crucial principles of academic responsibility. Faculty must be involved in program design and approval, but ways must be found to do this in rather less time than the many weeks and months usually consumed by the traditional academic review process. There are any number of ways in which this can be done. Some institutions have found it useful to delegate the collective faculty responsibility to a representative committee that meets frequently and can act quickly. Other campuses have moved from a policy of prior review to a post-audit mode in which courses and programs can be initiated without delay on a trial basis, subject to later review. There are other approaches as well, that are intermediate between the traditional lengthy process and an equally undesirable alternative in which programs are offered without academic oversight.

The question of admission is relevant only to credit-carrying offerings. The dilemma between the corporate desire to have a program open to all appropriate employees and the institutional insistence on degree standards can be resolved quite easily if admission to a credit course is kept separate from matriculation as a degree candidate, the latter being conditional on successful completion of one or more courses. Rapid and flexible registration at times and in ways other than those appropriate for traditional college students need present no major problem.

Adaptability of time, place, and format is so obviously necessary that it requires little amplification. There are evident limits to such adaptability to which the corporate clients need to be sensitive. It is also necessary to examine the relative advantages of the convenience of an on-site location with the countervailing advantages of an on-campus program that allows access to libraries and mixing of students from different backgrounds and occupations. A number of corporations have found that their employees prefer the latter, in spite of considerable additional cost and time for travel. These are issues that need to be worked out in collaboration with industry.

The necessary flexibility and adaptability can be considerably enhanced by the proper application of educational technology. A great deal can be done by imaginative use of televised material, cable, microwave transmission or physically transported video cassettes, coupled with the opportunity to question the instructor via telephone. The coming years will no doubt witness a rapid development of computer-assisted and computer-managed instruction and the use of video discs. Properly used, these will considerably enhance the ability of a faculty to reach out to a wide variety of sites.

In recent years, a number of universities have been very successful in the distribution of video-taped courses for managers and for technical professionals. The relatively advanced level of these offerings and the strong motivation of the students involved make it quite possible to use comparatively simple methods of production, such as the "talking head" or, preferably, the recording of an actual class session with one camera focused on the instructor and the second on the overhead projector or other graphic device.

Different methods are currently being used for distribution and feedback. Some institutions, such as the University of Massachusetts at Amherst, record actual classes on tape. These are duplicated and transported physically to different industrial locations, where they are shown as often as necessary. Questions are phoned in to the instructor at pre-arranged telephone office hours. This is obviously less desirable than being able actually to ask questions during the class. That is possible when the course is broadcast live to various sites, with telephone hookups back to the originating classroom allowing for direct interposition by any participating students.

Stanford University pioneered a system of Tutored Video-taped Instruction (TVI) which is now also used elsewhere. In this system, videotapes of classroom instruction are also distributed but they are shown at the industrial site only in the presence of a tutor. These tutors are chosen from the company's staff or from a local educational institution. They are familiar with the material and have themselves received brief training sessions in the use of televised materials, the conduct of discussions, and other pedagogic issues. The showing of the tape can be interrupted at any time for questions and discussion. A full description of the system and its outcomes is given by Gibbons (1977).

The Illinois Institute of Technology uses microwave transmission to broadcast a variety of engineering courses that can either be shown live or recorded at the remote site for use at various later times. Courier service ensures regular collection of written work with fast turn-around times (see Guralnick, 1981).

The Schools of Engineering at twenty-one universities have formed the national Association for Media-Based Continuing Education for Engineers which is currently developing plans for a National Technological University. The consortial effort will provide a variety of graduate degree programs, as well as individual courses by means of satellites (see Fitch, 1982).

Another consortium involved in industrial outreach is the Association for Higher Education in North Texas, which involves seventeen colleges and universities in the Dallas–Fort Worth area. Nine of these are connected to the TAGER Television network which uses point-to-point microwave transmission as well as satellites to distribute a wide variety of educational programs to businesses and industry throughout the region (Peters, 1982). Other examples of effective use of telecommunication for the delivery of employer-sponsored education can be cited, but in general this is still quite limited.

The rapid proliferation of municipal cable systems with high channel capacities will soon provide other possibilities to link institutions of higher education with small as well as large work places—or even with the homes of individual employees. Other, even more sophisticated technology appears to be just around the corner. The programmable video disc provides a substantial potential for a wide variety of instruction, particularly once the cost of producing a master disc decreases. Each successive generation of computers and the proliferation of microprocessors will inevitably lead to expanding use of computer-assisted and computer-managed instruction. It is, in fact, quite likely that employer-sponsored instruction, with the possibility of corporate support for the development of software and the acquisition of equipment, will accelerate the use of educational technology for "traditional" instruction.

If colleges and universities are to assume a greater role in providing employee education, they will have to make substantial changes in policies and procedures regarding faculty activity. A striking paradox characterizes the current situation. On the one hand, it is quite evident that relatively little of such instruction is provided through contract or other arrangements directly with the colleges and universities. On the other hand, all signs point to a substantial use of their faculties as designers and/or instructors of programs. Faculty members are either engaged directly by the corporate client as individual consultants, or they work for the third-party vendors who have the contract to design and deliver instruction. As mentioned earlier, the existing surveys of faculty consulting activities do not separate this kind of service from other categories, such as the provision of technical or management advice (Linnell, 1982). It is therefore not possible to estimate how much employer-sponsored instruction is in fact provided by college or university faculty, but the amount appears to be appreciable.

If this is indeed the case, it is an encouraging sign for higher education. It shows that in spite of much criticisim, the business world continues to value the knowledge and expertise of academics. At the same time, substantial use of individual faculty members as consultants underscores the importance of finding ways to provide this service more easily through institutional channels. Corporate clients at this time tend to bypass these channels because of all the procedural barriers mentioned earlier. They find it so much simpler, quicker, and hassle-free to turn directly to the individual faculty member. However, this is a disadvantage to the business clients in that they need to rely on informal networks, third-party vendors, or word of mouth to identify the most appropriate instructors to fill their educational needs.

Both employers and the academic institutions would be better served if mechanisms existed that would make faculty available through institutional channels on a flexible basis, as quickly and as easily as is now possible under consulting arrangements. Corporations could relinquish the burden of doing their own talent search and of carrying out their own detailed oversight and quality control of each individual workshop or course. By turning to the college or university, they would shift these responsibilities to the institution whose collective reputation and continuing relationship to the client would be at stake.

Flexibility of faculty participation is closely related to the broader issue of financing educational activities. Much of this chapter is based on the view that the modern college and university deals with a continuum of clienteles and that it no longer makes sense to divide the range of instruction arbitrarily into "regular" and "continuing" education. Unfortunately, this distinction without a difference is in part maintained by archaic public policies that force the two into fundamentally separate funding and budgeting modes. That is no longer appropriate. The continuous range of instructional activities is associated with a wide variety of funding sources. The dividing lines between what should be publicly subsidized and what should be self-supporting should no longer be drawn rigidly along an artificial line based on the age of the student and the time of instruction.

A full discussion of this complex issue goes beyond the scope of the present volume, which is limited basically to a call for optimal flexibility. If higher education is to realize its full potential in the development and maintenance of human capital, and if it is to participate more substantially in employer-sponsored education, there needs to be less rigidity in the separation between those instructional activities that are publicly supported and those that are not, and between teaching that is on-load and teaching that is provided on an overtime and extra compensation basis. At times, particularly in fields where traditional enrollment is decreasing, faculty may be readily available to provide instruction to employees as part of their regular teaching load, and there may even be occasions when it may be both cost-effective and pedagogically sound to mix different categories of students. There must be flexibility with regard to workload in other ways as well. Employee programs rarely fit into conventional molds of meeting so many times a week for fourteen or fifteen weeks. They may be shorter or longer, consist of half a dozen weekend sessions or concentrated into intensive immersion during a few days. It is essential to facilitate faculty participation by developing workload equivalents.

Furthermore, faculty members who provide off-campus instruction need to be compensated for travel expenses and, in some appropriate fashion, consideration also ought to be given to the travel time.

In some fields faculty may be available only on an overtime basis. This is most likely to be the case in those areas where faculty currently provide outside instructional services as consultants. Finding ways of channeling this through the academic institution would provide the institution itself with some direct benefit as well as a measure of control with regard to the consulting activities of its faculty. The privilege to engage in consulting is well established and time honored. It benefits not only the individual faculty member, but also, even under present arrangements, the institution by providing a direct channel of communication and feedback with the outside world. It would therefore be inappropriate to eliminate the practice of consulting. However, the current mode under which consulting is done entirely outside of institutional channels has serious shortcomings.

When a corporation or a consulting firm employs a faculty member on a per diem basis, it obtains the services of this individual at marginal cost and without having to pay the indirect, overhead expenses of the institution that furnishes the faculty member with a basic salary, office and research facilities, health insurance, and other fringe benefits. Should there not be some corporate contribution to these expenses, just as there would be if the corporation contracted to have a research project carried out by the faculty member? There are several conceivable ways in which the current practice could be modified without the loss of income to the consulting faculty, while yet assuring some reimbursement of indirect costs to the institution. The simplest approach would be to treat consultation in the same way that on-campus research or technical assistance activities are treated. It might be agreed that consultation fees would include an appropriate overhead charge (smaller than for on-campus projects) that would be either paid directly to the institution by the corporation or channeled through the consulting faculty member. A modification that would not actually involve the individual faculty member would be to request a direct contribution by a corporation in return for access to any number of faculty consultants—an arrangement somewhat analogous to the usual formulation for industrial support of joint industry-university research efforts.

A second approach would be to develop a "practice plan" similar to those currently used by almost every medical school for their clinical faculty. There are many variants to such a plan, but under all of them, the institution collects fees for patient service, and in most cases, returns to the faculty an amount that is calculated on a sliding scale. This maintains a substantial incentive and reward for the faculty member while also providing support for the institution.

The third approach is a very traditional one: it is that of the land grant institutions in providing the consulting services of their faculty and extension specialists. It is understood that a certain portion of such an individual's assignment is to be available for various forms of consultation. This provides great flexibility and availability. Similar arrangements exist in many Labor Studies Centers, the staff of which provide a wide variety of instruction. There are other examples as well. Common to all of them is the view of the "consultation" as an integral part of a faculty member's work load that does not lead to additional compensation.

It would be neither equitable nor politically feasible to institute this third model as it stands, particularly at this time when academic compensations do not keep pace with inflation. It is possible, however, to envision modifications that would result in appropriate income for the individual faculty members. A number of engineering schools have established centers for technical consultation that provide for this, and such arrangements could be expanded to include instructional services.

The entire issue is one that is at once sufficiently important and sufficiently complex to warrant being explored in concert by the academic community and the corporate sector.

The Need for Shared Authority and Dialogue

The changes in academic procedures and policies suggested in the above section of this chapter will considerably enhance the opportunities of academic institutions to provide a larger portion of employer-sponsored education. But those changes are not sufficient. Needed are further adaptations that go to the very heart of the academic enterprise. One is the urgent requirement that faculties abandon their traditional way of designing educational programs in splendid isolation, with little or no input from anyone outside the academy. Colleges and universities must learn to work together with employers in defining educational needs and in developing appropriate content and format. That so little of this occurs creates a good deal of resentment among business and industry officials, particularly those involved in the training and education of employees. They are faced time and again with what they view as an unwillingness of academics to sit down and discuss needs and approaches. They accuse faculties of being arrogant and insensitive to external realities. Employers understandably prefer to develop their own programs or to turn to third-party vendors whom they consider more responsive to their clients' desires.

Bridging this undercurrent of reproach and hostility must be a high priority for academic institutions interested in developing closer relationships with corporate clients. It is important for both sides to understand the difficulty and delicacy of finding the proper degree of cooperation. On the one hand, the input of the employer must be more than advisory. There needs to be a real sharing of authority. The external sponsor of educational programs must have a real voice in the determination of content.

On the other hand, the necessary sharing of authority with regard not only to what programs are needed, but also to what they should contain does not diminish the inescapable responsibility of a faculty and an academic institution for the quality and standards of their educational offerings, be they for credit or not. There is no valid way in which a college or university can evade this responsibility with the excuse that program content was developed jointly with external clients. Thus, a mode of cooperation must be found which imposes on academic institutions the difficulty of having to share authority without relinquishing responsibility.

Both partners in the dialogue must be sensitive to this. The corporate client must recognize the persistent responsibility of the academic partner and must be willing to make certain accommodations. These are most likely to consist of allowing programs to be broadened from a narrow emphasis on certain specific and practical skills to include more background and more theoretical understanding. A subsequent chapter describes some aspects of existing employer-sponsored programs about which questions can be raised. One of these is the extent to which such programs are narrowly defined, specifically relevant to a particular task or an immediate set of circumstances and with a very limited range of applicability. This may be most cost-effective in the short term, and indeed is very appropriate to many training needs for which lengthy background discussions would be neither useful nor germane. However, the reduction of instruction into small and essentially self-contained modules may well reduce the potential benefit of cumulative knowledge. Individual instructional units are less likely to be able to build on what has been learned before. In the long run, this may lead to wasteful repetition. It is therefore quite probable that a willingness of the employers to accommodate academic insistence on reasonable breadth may ultimately be to their own advantage.

At the same time, faculties must critically examine their own criteria of academic quality, and separate those that are intrinsically valid and defensible from those that are merely customary. Again, it is important to break the mold of "the way we have always done this." The typical academic tendency is to approach every subject from basic principles and to insist that these be thoroughly understood. Someone once described a detective novel written by the typical faculty member as starting with chapters on the ten commandments and the Babylonian code of laws, continuing with sections on the further development of jurisprudence in the Western world, the U.S. Constitution, the existing judicial system, the organization of the police, and finally ending with a description of the crime. The solution is left to the reader. This may constitute a slight exaggeration of the organization of the typical college course, but it contains enough truth to justify substantial criticism and to call for a very basic reexamination of the traditional academic approach.

In short, the necessary cooperation requires, on both sides, a great deal of sensitivity and much willingness to be flexible. Cross (1981) stated this very well in a paper that described a number of examples of different types of cooperation. At one extreme there are those relationships in which the employer's input is little more than token. Some kind of "advisory committee" meets sporadically and has little real impact. At the other extreme there exist instances in which some academic institutions lend their name and their credit to programs that are completely designed and delivered by business or industry, essentially without faculty involvement. After discussing the problems and limitations of the various models of cooperation, Cross adds:

> Hard as it may be to do so, establishing mutually supportive partnerships with industry seems to be an essential task on the new frontier. Higher education has much to learn about being a good partner. Reducing potential in-

dustrial partners to the status of junior partners whose
task it is to offer support without criticism is not likely to
result in a constructive or lasting relationship. Neither is
selling our soul for a mess of short-range benefits. But
establishing partnerships based on mutual trust and respect and a careful consideration of what each has to
offer is a pathway that seems clearly indicated on the new
frontier. The potential partners are many, and some
colleges are well along the road to forging promising
new partnerships. [p. 6]

The shape of these partnerships will vary widely, depending
on a variety of circumstances. In many situations it is best to develop close working relationships between a specific professional school or even a single department, on the one hand, and
on the other, each one of a number of large employers located
near the institution. Depending on the degree of competition
among the latter, it might be desirable gradually to amalgamate
these into a cooperative mechanism involving all similar enterprises in the region. There will be other cases in which it
makes more sense to develop a dialogue between the academic
institution as a whole and one or more employers, and perhaps
even to move toward a relationship involving a consortium of
colleges with a group of external clients.

The last is particularly valuable in a region such as New
England, which contains a large number and wide variety of
colleges and universities as well as a high concentration of
businesses and industries of varying size. In such a situation,
there are major opportunities for business-education collaboration, but, paradoxically, it provides also a source of difficulty.
The sheer number of prospective providers and potential users
of educational services is so great that it is difficult for any one
institution or any one enterprise to know where to start in developing constructive relationships. This is particularly true for
smaller colleges and even truer for smaller businesses. Men-
tion was made in an earlier chapter of the disproportionate
scarcity of employer-sponsored education in enterprises em-

ploying less than 500 individuals. These constitute more than 90 percent of all businesses and, together, employ more than a third of the labor force, yet appear to account for less than a fifth of the total expenditures for employee education. Clearly, the smaller enterprises cannot afford the staff and the organization to undertake adequate educational programs on an independent basis.

Joint efforts are therefore of great importance. A possible approach is to develop a third-party brokerage mechanism. One such effort is the Corporate-Education Exchange which has been initiated in the Boston area under the joint sponsorship of a number of businesses and educational institutions. (For information, write to: Corporate-Education Exchange, 100 Federal Street, Boston, MA 02110.)

In its initial stages, the Exchange is concentrating on bringing about working relationships at the operating level in order to provide three benefits: market access, reciprocal information, and market aggregation. With regard to access, it is clear that the brokerage can help both educational institutions and employers to make initial contact. This is likely to lead to savings in cost and energy on both sides as compared with individual approaches. The Exchange can also establish relationships between types of institutions and categories of employers who may never have communicated before and are very unfamiliar with each other. It is quite possible, for example, that a personnel manager of a bank who is very familiar with the regional business schools may be at a loss as to the best source for programs in English as a second language.

The ability of the brokerage mechanism to make useful connections between potential providers and users depends of course on its ability to accumulate and make available information about available resources and existing needs. The Exchange will accumulate as complete an inventory as possible of institutional strengths as well as of enterprise requirements in its region.

In addition, the Corporate-Education Exchange can help businesses to place small numbers of employees with those other enterprises that have the same educational needs, encourage colleges to develop programs that could not be justified for a single client, and also to pool resources when the needs of a single employer exceed the capability of a single institution in terms either of numbers or of scope.

With a track record of success in bringing about more cooperation at the operational level, and as participants from both sectors get to know each other better and reach a reasonable level of mutual confidence, a brokerage mechanism can lead to a more profound dialogue involving long-range policy and planning issues. Chapter 7 describes the great need for systematic cooperation with regard to human resource policy and planning between higher education and business, and involving government as well.

CHAPTER 5

A Reexamination of Professional Education

As stated in Chapter 4, many corporate executives feel that a substantial portion of employer-sponsored education is, for all intents and purposes, designed to remedy real or perceived shortcomings of the prior education and preparation acquired by the newly hired employees during their undergraduate or graduate years. In Lusterman's study, 27 percent of those canvassed believed that some or most of what they provide for their employees should really have been the responsibility of school or college (Lusterman, 1977, p. 63). If indeed this is the case, it is a very serious situation. In the first place, it suggests a wasteful duplication of effort for both employers and employees. Resources need to be devoted to make up for shortcomings for academic preparation for which a good deal of both time and money has already been spent. In the second place, if employers have reason to be dissatisfied with the pre-employment preparation that their work force obtained in colleges and universities, they will be understandably reluctant to turn to these institutions for further training for the employees.

The comments of employers, as well as the content of the programs most often provided for newly hired employees, clearly indicate what are considered the principal shortcomings of the academic preparation of our colleges and universities.

One almost universal complaint, all too familiar and all too valid, concerns the inability of individuals even with advanced degrees to express themselves clearly and concisely, orally or in writing. Graduates write badly, speak badly, and even listen badly. Corporations find this problem no less intractable than colleges and universities find it, and there is a tendency on the part of both constituencies to lay all the blame on the inadequacy of primary and secondary education. There is much truth in this, yet it is also clear that higher education must intensify its efforts with regard to its students' communication skills. The percentage of companies providing basic remedial education for their employees is too high (Table 2.9, p. 52).

The dissatisfaction of employers, however, goes well beyond unhappiness about inadequate basic skills. A substantial number of employers find our graduates inadequately prepared to be effective on the job. Employers as well as recent graduates are almost unanimous in criticizing the inadequate linkage in undergraduate and graduate education between theoretical analysis and practical experience. Most graduates have excessive difficulty making the transition from classroom to employment. They have mastered sophisticated techniques and acquired much factual knowledge, but often find that their preparation is not directly applicable to the situations and the tasks they face in the work place. Some of the corporate complaints on this score are exaggerated: one cannot expect academic institutions to prepare "turnkey" products that can hit the ground running without any on-the-job training and acclimatization. But the current conceptual gap between campus and work place is much too wide.

The widening of this gap is most probably a consequence of the assimilation of professional schools into the university which was mentioned in Chapter 3. For many years, several academic observers of the development of professional education during the past decades have been pointing out that this was happening. For example, Jencks and Riesman (1968) discussed "the professional schools' tendency either to affiliate with a multipurpose university or to expand into one" and warned that "the affiliation of professional schools with universities probably encourages those who educate future professionals to take a more academic and less practical view of what students need to know" (p. 252). The authors further described law schools that "pay almost no attention to their students' non-intellectual development, even though this will be critically important to most students' subsequent career achievement" (p. 252). They also wrote that "engineering professors . . . are usually interested in turning out men with skills appropriate to teachers of engineering; they simply take it for granted that these skills will also be appropriate to the practice of engineering. In many cases, of course, they are right. But in many cases they are probably wrong" (p. 253). A similar point was made by Hughes (1973, pp. 288–89) in describing the prestige system in teaching professionals.

These attitudes lead to a "divergence between professional training and professional practice" (Jencks and Riesman, p. 253). For many years, complaints about this were voiced only privately by both employers and college graduates. But during 1982 and ever since there have appeared in the press a veritable chorus of statements that *at both the undergraduate and the graduate level, university education fails to produce competent and effective professionals.*

A set of articles in the *New York Times*, under the heading "What's New at Harvard Business School," contained the following:

> But despite the addition of the course [on labor and personnel issues] . . . some professors grumble that Harvard's business education needs a more fundamental overhaul. They share a nagging doubt: That some research is getting too academic and that Harvard may be neglecting to teach managers how to put into effect the strategies which they develop. [1982, p. C21]

More recently, additional complaints about the current state of management education have appeared in several places. An article about the Stanford Business School complains that MBA students are taught to analyze problems but not to manage companies. *Business Week* quotes a chief executive of a major corporation as saying, in a similar vein: "We've created a terrible philosophy in our business schools. We've created middle managers who do not know how to run the things they're supposed to know how to run" (Browne, 1983, p. 80).

Reich (1983) complains that:

more and more, the career ambitions of America's best students have turned to professions that allow them to continue attending to symbols, from quiet offices equipped with telephones, a Telex and a good secretary. The world of truly productive people, engaged in the untidy and difficult struggle with real production problems, is becoming alien to America's best and brightest. [p. 160]

But blame does not rest on the academic institutions alone: external expectations have changed. *Business Week* also explains:

For two decades, the job market placed a premium on market researchers, planners and financial experts whose knowledge was largely confined to analysis, theory and number manipulation. No longer. Now companies demand managers who contribute to the bottom line and who possess the skills needed for the increasingly complex job of running a business. [1983, p. 76]

Hayes and Abernathy at the Harvard Business School were among the first to point out the basic weaknesses of what they called "the new management orthodoxy": "American managers have increasingly relied on principles which prize analytical detachment and methodological elegance over insight, based on experience, into the subtleties and complexities of strategic decisions" (Hayes and Abernathy, 1980, p. 70). Since then, a growing number of books and articles have appeared that call for a fundamental change in the American approach to management (see, for example, Reich, 1983; Peters and Waterman, 1982). Some are written by academics, some by businessmen, still others by consultants. They vary with regard to specific recommendations but agree on the basic issue: the era of scientific management must give way to a more flexible approach. We will return to this issue in the next chapter.

Criticism is increasingly being heard about other professional areas as well. An article in *Fortune* magazine complained that in engineering education an emphasis on abstract problems and research has replaced "hands-on" experience and practical subjects (Main, 1982). As a result, graduating engineers have great difficulty when they are first employed. When faced with the responsibility of turning out a product, they find themselves ill prepared to handle the task. An editorial in *Science* expressed the same warning, and suggested that engineering education should model itself on medical preparation and include clinical training (Abelson, 1982). But medical education has itself, once again, come under considerable criticism. The American Association of Medical Colleges has embarked on a three-year study of the medical curriculum because:

> Medical students are being overwhelmed by scientific detail at the expense of basic skills and a regard for human needs.... Undergraduate as well as medical school students are being driven to absorb an enormous amount of science at the sacrifice of just about everything else. [Blair, 1982, p. 3]

A common theme links all of these statements, as well as a number of similar ones that have appeared in recent months: the current approach to higher education, particularly professional training, is too abstract, too theoretical, and at the same time too limited to purely cognitive content. Competence requires knowledge but transcends it. By and large, we provide our students with inadequate help to bridge the gap between theory and practice. We furnish them with a great deal of knowledge but pay too little attention to their ability to use this knowledge in a competent and effective fashion. As a result, corporate executives and other employers everywhere complain that the graduates of our professional schools do not function on the job without a considerable amount of further training.

It is very evident that the competence of college graduates would be significantly enhanced if courses of study at both the undergraduate and the graduate levels were to include periods of practical experience that go beyond the laboratory, the case study, the simulation, or the guided design. One or more of these pedagogic devices to demonstrate the practical application of theory is contained in most professional curricula. They are valuable, but by their very nature they fall short of providing students with the experience of a real work experience. In the academic exercises, problems are usually well defined, variables are limited, and the setting a closed framework. Reality is more messy.

Many undergraduate and graduate curricula do include external experiences through internships, clerkships, and other supervised clinical periods. The use of these experiential components has been limited by two factors. In some professional areas, particularly in law, clinical experience has long been suspect because it seemed to be lacking in rigor, and perhaps also because it harks back too much to the days when apprenticeship was an adequate road to legal practice. However, clinical practice in the law curriculum is now being considered even at Harvard. The second barrier is the tendency to cram all conceivable facts, figures, and theories into all curricula. New subjects and new courses keep being added, few are ever dropped, and in the competition for time slots in the curriculum, practical experiences often lose out.

In spite of such obstacles, the many successful examples of internships incorporated into professional curricula show that their use can and should be implemented much more widely. In some areas, such as medicine and other health professions, clinical periods are of course an essential part of education. Where they are not, practical periods have usually been most effective if they involve faculty and students together. The centers for technical consultation at a number of engineering schools that were discussed in Chapter 4 furnish excellent opportunities for such cooperation on a client's project.

The competition for time in the curriculum is largely avoided in full-fledged cooperative education programs where the succession of work experiences is usually added to the classroom components and results in a longer course of study toward the degree. Cooperative Education was begun at the University of Cincinnati in 1906 and grew moderately until the beginning of World War II. In 1942 there existed thirty successful programs. After the war there was a spurt, and cooperative education programs now exist in over one hundred community colleges, four-year institutions, and universities in the U.S. (CERC, 1978). Approximately 140,000 students and over 30,000 employers participate. These are truly impressive figures, yet they constitute only a small fraction of the total enrollment in higher education and the vast number of public and private employers.

All existing assessments of cooperative education programs indicate their value in allowing students to test their theoretical knowledge in a real working situation and to see whether it measures up to the expectations of the employer. Furthermore, participation in cooperative education makes significant contributions to the development of interpersonal competence, communication skills, and planning ability.

A different development that can also help to relate practical experience to theory is the trend in a growing number of prestigious business schools to give preferential admission or even to require at least two years of employment prior to enrollment in a graduate management program. However, the best programs of internships or cooperative education are limited unless the experiential component is integrated into all parts of the educational process. It must be linked to the theory; it should inform and illuminate what is taught in the classroom. Students and faculty alike must attempt to draw general conclusions from specific instances.

This will require a substantial change in the prevalent mode of instruction, which is predominantly deductive. At all levels of higher education, the common pedagogic approach is to begin with basic principles and general theories, and to deduce from them the applications to practical circumstances. Many faculty members will find it difficult to proceed in the opposite direction and to work with their students in order to induce generalized conclusions from specific experiences. Yet it is a much needed change. Unfortunately very little attention has been paid to this until now, even in the extensive literature on experiential learning. Hatala (1982) suggests that a problem-solving model of professional study may provide the vehicle for effectively integrating experiential learning into traditional classroom teaching. He stops short of addressing what form this integration should take.

The systematic integration of practical experiences into the professional curriculum would not only affect pedagogic approach but is likely to lead to even more profound and un-settling changes. Students can learn from a critical examination of most actual situations that the "real world" is both more complex and more ambiguous than the typical textbook illus-trations of professional technique and disciplinary methodolo-gy. If properly incorporated into the curriculum, periods of practical experience as well as good case studies in the classroom can test theory against practice and illustrate not only the power but also the limitations of the former. It will indicate that most complex situations do not fit neatly into the pursuit of any single discipline and are not susceptible to the ready application of an isolated professional technique.

One of the most serious and most justified criticisms of aca-demic education is its lack of attention to problem solving. The discipline has become its own end rather than a means toward the understanding and resolution of complex situations. Pro-fessional schools have tended to become collections of graduate departments, each pursuing the development of its own dis-cipline rather than joining with others to enhance the effec-tiveness of the profession. Greater emphasis in the curriculum on analyzing real problems will force faculties to broaden their approach so as to enable students to bring to bear more than one discipline and more than one technique. The students may learn that the development of theory necessarily involves a number of simplifications as well as substantial narrowing and specialization. Actual situations are inevitably "messy," ambiguous, and subject to conflicting interpretations so that no single set of disciplinary tools quite fits. Several different perspectives are needed simultaneously.

Clearly there is a limit to the ability of any one individual to apply the methodologies of various disciplines to a single situation. No one can become a jack of all trades with adequate expertise in many fields. Because of this, a greater emphasis on problem solving can also lead to more of a team approach. Achieving this would improve another serious shortcoming of academic education as perceived by employers: on the job, most employees will work in groups or teams whose members will bring different skills and expertise to the complex tasks at hand. Kidder's account of the development of a new computer in *The Soul of a New Machine* (1981) is an excellent illustration of the importance of team work in high technology. And Reich (1983) points out the importance in modern industry of integrating individuals' skills "into a group whose collective capacity becomes something more than the simple sum of its members' skills" (p. 135). Yet the entire pedagogic approach in higher education focuses on the individual. In setting tasks and in evaluating performance and achievement, we only know how to deal with one person's effort. It will be very difficult to change this individual orientation, but a greater emphasis on complex problem solving is likely to help.

Thus a more experiential and inductive approach to education will require—and may facilitate—more emphasis on problem-solving skills as well as on the ability to work as members of a team. It is also likely to stimulate yet another broadening element in professional education. Analyzing actual situations and exploring alternative decisions will very quickly indicate the importance of understanding the social, economic, and political contexts of a given situation. At the beginning of this chapter, many critics of existing professional education and also of current management approaches were quoted. They are clearly concerned about more than practical applications of techniques and the gap between theory and reality. They realize that actual situations are complex and that one cannot cope with them only with "analytical detachment and methodological elegance." Reality, as we have already emphasized, is messy. It involves the interplay of all kinds of social, political, and economic currents and cross-currents. Managers and other professionals in government, business, and industry must increasingly be able to cope with this, and clearly this requires a *broad* education. As *Business Week* states: generalists, not specialists are needed (Browne, 1983, p. 50).

This constitutes a major departure from an earlier infatuation with professionalism and analysis. Furthermore, the calls for breadth of understanding extend to lower and lower levels of corporate and public-sector hierarchies. In fact, the hierarchies are being replaced by "flatter" organizational patterns (Reich, 1983, p. 136). This has been considerably speeded up by the recent recession. One of its most marked effects on corporate structures has been a widespread elimination of middle-level positions and an accelerated trend toward greater decentralization. Decision making is being increasingly delegated to lower professional and managerial echelons. Thus, individuals in even relatively modest supervisory positions now need more than narrow technical knowledge. As their role shifts from merely supplying information to higher echelons toward greater responsibility, their need to understand the broad context of their activities will also increase.

These requirements were recently the subject of yet another report by the influential Conference Board, authored by the same person who carried out the important study of employer-sponsored education. The new report is somewhat misleadingly entitled, "Managerial Competence: The Public Affairs Aspect" (Lusterman, 1981), but goes well beyond public affairs concerns. It points out that "knowledge of society and of the public policy process . . . is deemed essential to the managerial role" (p. 5), and agrees with other critics that "traditional business goals and incentives have been antithetical to the cultivation either of interest or competence in the public affairs function" (p. 7). The report calls for more emphasis in employer-sponsored programs on understanding social and political as well as economic factors. It does not address the implications for professional preparation, but clearly furnishes yet another argument for substantial change. We need to reverse the trend in management education and in other professional curricula that are not only theoretical but also narrowly defined. We must broaden the content of professional education to enable individuals to cope more effectively with a messy, complex, and difficult reality.

This, rather than providing some spurious cultural veneer, should be the goal of including the traditional subjects of liberal arts as a much more important part of professional education. Traditional liberal arts subjects are not ends in themselves. The purpose of understanding the context in which problems are defined and decisions are taken cannot be accomplished by adding a few survey courses into the early years of the professional curriculum. Instead, there is a great need to provide in later years, much as Daniel Bell (1966) has suggested, a number of specially designed seminars that are designed to place the professional activity into a broader context. This broadening of professional education will also require growing collaboration between all component units of the comprehensive university in the review and revision of courses and curricula. It is also an important reason for centralized coordination of the working relationships with employers in developing employee education. And ultimately it may lead at least to a partial blurring of that unfortunate and inappropriate distinction between "liberal" and "vocational" studies.

All of these modifications of the professional curriculum may help to lead to even more fundamental changes. The early sixties were an era of unquestioned acceptance of professionalism. This was epitomized in a special issue on the professions of the distinguished periodical *Daedalus*. In its preface, the editors could state that "Everywhere in American life, the professions are triumphant . . . [the] dream of a professionally run society has never been closer to realization" (Lynn, 1963, p. 92). Many subsequent events have punctured that euphoria, and in recent years there has been a mounting chorus of criticism of professional activity. A growing number and range of observers have voiced the view that technique has become dominant and self-serving. The French philosopher Ellul expresses perhaps an extreme, almost Luddite view in stating that "Technique is autonomous. . . . [It] elicits and conditions social, political and economic change. . . . Man himself has become overpowered by technique and become its object" (1964, p. 133).

In a more moderate fashion, Morison (1966) speaks of "the tendency . . . to proceed toward whatever is economically and technically possible without regard to other considerations of interest and value" (p. 223). In Schein's (1972) important critique of professional education, he pointed out that:

> professionals are so specialized that they have become unresponsive to certain classes of social problems. . . .
> . . . professionals have become unresponsive to the need of many classes of ultimate clients or users of their services, working instead for the organization which employs them." [p. 59]

Along a similar vein, Argyris and Schön (1974) describe the prevalent model of professional behavior as unilateral and essentially coercive. They argue that it tends to distort the context and to define problems in a way that assures the predictable working of technique, rather than finding the proper modification and combination of approaches that would enable the actual situation to be resolved in an optimal fashion. Many others have advanced similar arguments.

This issue requires very thorough examination which is likely to lead to profound changes in the definition of professional activity (Schön, 1983a), and in turn to suggest sweeping modifications of professional education (Joiner, 1980; Schön, 1983b). But even the limited step of including more analysis of prior experience and actual situations in the curriculum can have beneficial effects within this broader context. It can, for example, lead to the highly important recognition that often the most difficult and the most ambiguous aspect of professional activity is the *definition* of the problem, not its solution. It is in the process of setting the parameters and of articulating the objectives that choices need to be made among what almost inevitably are competing values of comparable importance. Much has been written lately about the importance of "teaching values," a task that is both difficult and indeed highly questionable. Teaching values all too easily deteriorates into indoctrination. But irrespective of one's views about the teaching of values, there can be general agreement on the paramount importance of helping students to understand that just about every decision involves values. Choices among competing goals and purposes require the application of subjective values. This happens in all kinds of ways and at all possible levels. In small, local decisions as well as at the national level, the enhancement of employment may conflict with environmental considerations, and the right of the individual may conflict with the collective safety or convenience of the community. Exercising the rights of one group may place restraints on the activity of another. Seniority rights often stand in opposition to the goals of affirmative action, and skyrocketing health-care costs are already forcing some countries to make conscious choices between costly transplant surgery for the few against better preventive and primary care for the many.

The actual choices facing the individual are not always so profound, but even in the most mundane situations, the definition of the task and the setting of the problem more often than not involve a trade-off among competing values. Our current approach to professional education, with its strong emphasis on purely cognitive elements and on the predominance of technique, tends to ignore this. Again, there are babies in this bath water. The necessary reform should not denigrate the development of cognitive and methodological skills. These continue to be essential, and we must still require professionals to have a substantial mastery of technique. But the educational process needs also to include substantial emphasis on understanding the *limitations* of these elements in order to ensure that they at all times remain means toward a greater end, rather than an autonomous, self-serving, and ultimately destructive system.

Achieving such an understanding involves, also, a grasp of

the human elements involved in every working situation. One of the strongest criticisms expressed by employers about professional education is its lack of emphasis on interpersonal relations and organizational effectiveness. Indeed, one finds that a considerable portion of employer-sponsored programs, both inhouse and through a variety of third-party vendors ranging from the National Training Laboratories to Dale Carnegie, is devoted to such affective topics. Employers place considerable importance on the ability of their employees to function effectively within a complex organization, and would like more emphasis on this in the academic preparation of prospective employees. There is little doubt that part of the necessary reform of professional education must be the inclusion of some development of affective, interpersonal, and other behavioral skills that are pertinent to professional activity. The optimal amount and the best approach, however, are far from clear. Some middle ground needs to be found between the typical academic tendency to have courses in theories of human and organizational behavior, and the current mode prevalent in employer-sponsored programs that are reminiscent of the "touchy-feely" activities that swept many college campuses in the sixties. As mentioned earlier, cooperative education programs and other experiential learning tend to enhance the interpersonal skills of participating students. They may constitute the most promising approach to this issue.

All of this adds up to the need for a profound review and far-reaching revision of higher education at both the graduate and undergraduate levels. It is a call for making all of it more germane to the future activities of the students, yet paradoxically, it is also a call for breadth and for more truly liberal education than is now found either in the professional curricula or in the arts and sciences.

The ability to deal with others and to function in a complex organization constitutes only a small part of the breadth needed in professional education. Every indicator suggests that individuals at almost every level of public and private organizations have a growing need to grasp the complexities of their environment and to understand the role of their own work in a broader context. It is becoming increasingly clear that far more than narrow technical knowledge is essential for effectiveness on the job. Yet we persist in maintaining a gulf between "liberal" and "vocational" education. The separation manifests itself in a variety of ways. In universities throughout the country there is little communication between the colleges of arts and sciences, on the one hand, and the professional schools, on the other. Interest in general education occurs in cycles that are almost predictable in their regularity, but even when emphasis on breadth is at its peak, it is approached in terms of core curricula and distribution requirements that are considered to be quite distinct from the "disciplinary" or "vocational" portion of the curriculum. There is much discussion of the "whole person," but rarely if ever is there an exploration of the relationship between the students' majors and their general education. Occasional lip service is paid to the basic point that in the development of an individual for effective activity—on the job and as a citizen—one cannot meaningfully distinguish between "vocational" and "liberal" components. It is high time to translate this from a pious statement into educational reality, and to develop curricula that truly combine the two into an integral whole (Lynton, 1982c; Clecak, 1977). We will return to this point in the concluding portion of the book.

The point here is that there is a reciprocal relationship between substantial changes in professional education, and a strengthened role of colleges and universities in employer-sponsored programs. The dissatisfaction of employers with the inappropriateness of the academic preparation of their newly hired employees adds to the reluctance of corporations to turn to higher education for further employee development. Because of this dissatisfaction and the consequent reluctance, it is urgently necessary to take a searching and self-critical look at professional education and to initiate a number of basic changes. At the same time, these changes will be greatly eased if there is closer collaboration between the academy and the world of work. Systematic and vigorous moves by higher education to establish closer ties with employers are likely to trigger a positive and accelerating feedback mechanism that can substantially improve the quality of professional education. At the same time, as will be discussed in the next chapter, it can also help to influence the nature of employer-sponsored education.

On the academic side, it is quite possible that the greatest impact of enhanced interaction between the spheres of education and employment will be on the faculty who are so central to the enterprise. It is easy to theorize about the adaptations that should take place in our colleges and universities, ranging from minor modifications to a fundamental rethinking of professional activity. It is even relatively easy for academic administrators to design the necessary organizational and procedural adaptations. But substantive change in an academic institution can only be brought about by the faculties. Academic institutions, especially universities, are highly non-hierarchical organizations. Their central characteristics and priorities depend largely on what the faculty considers important. Changes of the core of the institutions by administrative or external fiat are virtually impossible, and indeed this high degree of autonomy is a vital element in the strength and purposes of higher education in a democratic society. But this autonomy also results in the problem that faculties, collectively, are highly conservative bodies, difficult to move. An earlier chapter discussed how little the basic nature of our universities has changed after Sputnik in spite of drastic changes both in size and in purpose. Universities undertook a much more varied task, but on the whole the new or expanded activities occurred by adding peripheral units and a considerable number of non-academic staff (see, for example, Smelser, 1974). The core faculty itself continued to focus its energies and to shape its value system on carrying out basic research and teaching future professionals in the discipline (Schein, 1972; Hughes, 1973).

In recent years one can point to an increasing number of indications that faculty interest is becoming considerably more responsive to external needs in both their teaching and their professional and scholarly activities. Interest and good will, however, are not enough. The necessary transformations are made difficult by the profound isolation of many faculty members—even in the professional schools—from the realities of the external world. Greater involvement of higher education in employee education can have a far-reaching impact on this faculty isolation. It can bring about closer ongoing contact between faculty members and practitioners in the field, and can result in a much broader and better-informed perspective on the nature of professional education.

One additional issue must be noted. The prevalent opinion among employers is that most college and university faculty do not know how to teach experienced adults, and, in many cases, are unwilling to learn. Their pedagogic style is basically authoritarian, an approach that may be suitable for eighteen-year-old freshmen but is less appropriate for an older and experienced manager or other professional returning to the classroom. The important subject of the methodology of teaching adults has received a great deal of attention in recent years (see, for example, Peterson, 1983). The vast majority of faculty in our colleges and universities will probably pay as little attention to theoretical studies of the teaching of adults as they have to pedagogic theories for the traditional student cohort. But an effort must be made, at the very least, to become more sensitive to the needs as well as to the capacity of the adult learner. Older students—and indeed probably all students—can learn as much from each other as from the instructor, and can to a considerable extent proceed at their own pace if the latter becomes more of a facilitator and catalyst for learning rather than the sole source of *ex cathedra* enlightenment.

CHAPTER 6

Some Comments about Employer-Sponsored Education

AN EXTERNAL OBSERVER of employer-sponsored education needs to keep firmly in mind that the goals and the priorities of these activities are not the same as those of regular schooling in academic institutions. In that sense, Dunlop's much-quoted tag, "shadow system of education," is misleading. It suggests an inappropriate degree of similarity with the traditional educational system. There really are quite basic differences. In both the private and the public sectors, the main priority of employers must be the cost-effective operation of their enterprise. The development and renewal of employee skills are appropriate only to the extent to which they are consistent with this goal. By contrast, the educational system at all levels exists to foster individual development as a principal priority (Lynton, 1981b).

Academic observers do not always understand and appreciate this difference, in part because of the lack of communication and discussion between corporate trainers and college faculties on these issues. The latter have shown little or no interest or willingness to talk; the former have tended to form themselves into a self-contained group. This has resulted

111

in a professionalization of employee training and organizational development into a distinct vocation, with its own national associations, publications, meetings, and inevitably, its own jargon. Such a development has many advantages. It creates a network of information and of exchange of experience; it helps to translate arcane theoretical concepts into practical terms and applicable programs; and it provides legitimation and visibility to activities that are too often ignored. But there exists, as well, the danger that a profession will become a closed circle in which corporate trainers and external consultants reinforce each other without much disinterested criticism, and through which valid concepts may degenerate into catch phrases and simplistic mnemonics.

This danger—if it indeed exists—is heightened by the problem of how to evaluate any kind of education and training, corporate or collegiate. Except for programs that are intended to transmit some very specific skills that can be easily tested, it is already difficult to define the desired objectives, let alone to find reliable ways of assessing their achievement. What is the purpose of developing interpersonal skills? Is it to increase productivity or to improve quality control, to reduce organizational tensions, to enhance personal satisfaction and self-fulfillment? Any of the above, or all of them? Given these ambiguities, it is not surprising that in the corporate sector, as in the vast majority of colleges and universities, program evaluation appears to be limited to surveying participant response.

As a result of the lack of communication, as well as of the paucity of evaluation, comments by an academic observer of employer-sponsored education are made on the basis of limited and qualitative impressions. This should be kept in mind in reading the following remarks.

The Human Relations Component

A substantial portion of employer-sponsored activities consists of programs intended to enhance interpersonal relationships, teamwork, and organizational development. The emphasis on these human skills is, of course, to a considerable extent a response to the perceived inadequacy of professional preparation in our colleges and universities. It is a remedial effort made necessary by the lack of attention to human behavior and to affective skills in most academic programs. The need for interpersonal effectiveness is becoming more intense because of the growing organizational complexity of most modern enterprises, their use of increasingly sophisticated technology in many operations, and their involvement in a more and more complicated economic, political, and social environment. Schein (1977) among others, has pointed out that this paradoxically causes "increased dependence upon the very people which make up the organization." Management increasingly consists of "managing the *process* of decision making," which is essentially a human and interpersonal activity (Schein, 1977, pp. 2–3). More and more supervisors and operational managers are involved in this because of the marked trend toward decentralization in many large business organizations, with the locus of decisionmaking shifting to lower levels.

Further demands on interpersonal skills arise because corporate organizational patterns often consist of lateral as well as vertical relationships. During the seventies, a number of large corporations developed a so-called matrix organization as a way of combining a decisional format based on products with a format that relates the same function—such as marketing—for all products. Matrix structures also were used in certain technological firms as a way of organizing major developmental projects in which research must be closely related to several other management areas (see, for example, Janger, 1979). Since then, fully structured matrix management organizations have been largely abandoned because they turned out to be excessively cumbersome, although many industrial enterprises have retained some form of multidimensional organization. These multidimensional formats place even greater demands on the human skills of the individual than the more traditional hierarchical structure. When someone has multiple reporting relationships, when responsibility is not always matched with authority, and when cooperation and team effort are at a premium, personal behavior and relationships assume a special importance.

The strong emphasis on affective skills in employer-sponsored programs also reflects the "human relations" concern
with job satisfaction and personal fulfillment as factors in organizational effectiveness and productivity (MacGregor, 1960;
see also Peters and Waterman, 1982, pp. 89–103). In recent
years, much of this has become subsumed under the term
QWL, which stands for Quality of Work Life, a widespread
movement toward more participation by production and service workers in managerial decisions, restructuring jobs to be
less fragmented and to allow more pride in accomplishment,
and various other ways of improving worker satisfaction (see,
for example, Skrovan, 1980; Simmons and Mares, 1983).
Progress in these directions requires, on the one hand, that the
worker has a broad understanding beyond the technical skills
needed for a specific operation, and on the other hand, places
greater demands on the interpersonal skills of supervisors and
managers.

In view of all of these trends, it is therefore no wonder that
corporate training and development places a pervasive emphasis on affective and behavioral elements and faults higher education for its inadequate attention to them. The limited amount
of coursework dealing with organizational development and interpersonal relationships in the typical professional curriculum
is likely to be highly abstract, dealing more with general concepts and theories and of little help to the individual who is
soon to be faced with the actual human complexities of the
work place. One has the impression, however, that the corporate approach to these issues tends to go to an opposite extreme. Many of the pertinent employer-sponsored programs
(provided more often than not by third-party vendors) appear
to be almost totally affective, stressing sensitivity training and
group dynamics and making little attempt to draw general-
izations or to understand the process. Many of the sessions appear to have as their primary goal making participants feel better about themselves and their environment.

In their recent critique of current management approaches,
Peters and Waterman (1982) speak of the "silly excesses" of the
human relations school which "went off the deep end on T-

groups, bottom-up planning, democratic management and other forms of a make everyone happy work environment" (pp. 95–96). Elsewhere, Peters and Waterman criticize the "seemingly ubiquitous organization development movement, replete with team building, T-groups, conflict resolution and managerial grids" (p. 241). In their view and that of the many contemporary critics of management, these goals of the human relations movement are not wrong—quite the contrary. But Peters and Waterman, as well as the others, believe that human relations and organizational development have very little meaning unless they become an integral part of an overall management approach, rather than being a separate and unrelated add-on: "The overwhelming failure of the human relations movement was precisely its failure to be seen as a balance to the excesses of the rational model [of management]" (p. 95).

The dichotomy between "human relations" and "scientific management" is quite analogous to the equally artificial separation between the "liberal" and "vocational" components of educational programs. The widespread failure of general education is largely due to its apparent lack of relevance to the subject matter of the students' concentration and professional preparation. We will return to this issue.

The Importance of Breadth and Context

The lack of congruence between "human relations" and the prevalent approach to current management is mirrored in the striking contrast between the human skills component of employer-sponsored education and those programs that focus on technical competence. If the former appears to suffer from a certain lack of specificity and to be characterized principally by a desire to make people feel better about themselves, the latter are close to the opposite end of the spectrum. They derive directly from the classical Taylor approach of scientific management which relates the training of workers as directly as possible to a systematic analysis of their function into a number of component steps and processes (Taylor, 1947). Succinct descriptions of the applications of Taylor's ideas to education and to industry are found in Neumann (1979) and in Steinmetz (1980).

The more a developmental program is tied to a specific task, the narrower the definition of the end product of the learning process becomes. In the case of the application of Taylor's ideas to primary education, the performance objectives are both behavioral and functional. In work-place applications, the functional goals predominate. The development process becomes one of providing small increments of training in narrowly defined skills that have specific and immediate utility.

This applies to most employer-sponsored programs other than those that are directed at the development of interpersonal skills. Whether carried out in house or contracted externally, most of the developmental activities are narrowly defined, specifically relevant to a particular task or an immediate set of circumstances, and have a well-defined and limited application. It is training rather than education, if one attempts to distinguish between these two ambiguous terms. In their discussion of education in industry, Branscombe and Gilmore (1975) suggest a scale of parameters along which the distinction can be drawn. At the training end "lies measurability, narrowness of subject matter, relevance to a particular time and place, well defined range of use and efficiency of information transfer" (p. 226). The education end of the scale, by contrast, is characterized by "exposure to contrasting assumptions and points of view, the involvement of personal intellectual initiative, less constrained range of use even to uncertainty about its specific utility" (p. 227). The authors also point out that education, properly provided, is cumulative, whereas small units of training are apt to be independent.

These descriptions are stated in detail to underscore the obvious values of training. Relevance and utility should characterize all transmission of knowledge and information, and efficiency is certainly also generally desirable. Much of the very justified criticism of academic education is caused by its lack of these attributes. And they are certainly very appropriate to the purposes and priorities of the business sector which must, of necessity, operate under severe limitations of resources, particularly in terms of the time that supervisors, managers, and professionals can spend on formal developmental programs. Furthermore industry in this country is strongly oriented toward short-term profitability and the bottom line of quarterly financial statements. All of this demands that employer-sponsored development, on the whole, be cost-effective and able to show a relatively rapid return on investment. It is therefore not surprising that much of these activities can be characterized as training.

Indeed, the majority of individuals involved in the corporate human resource development effort consider and call themselves trainers. Their principal professional organization is the American Society for Training and Development (ASTD), which publishes a journal called *Training and Development Journal.* The academic tendency to denigrate training is viewed as yet another instance of arrogance. Failure to recognize the appropriateness of training to many of the needs of business and industry creates yet another barrier to effective cooperation between business and higher education.

However, even though short-term returns are understandably important to a profit-driven enterprise, long-term cost-effectiveness is also essential. When it comes to the development of a new model, the launching of a different product line, the construction of new physical facilities, or the purchase of equipment, long-term considerations are routinely balanced against immediate profitability. That is common business procedure in most aspects of corporate operation, yet it does not appear to be prevalent in the area of employee development. There, on the whole, immediate needs and quick return appear to be given far greater weight than deferred benefits.

Task analysis is very important, and indeed one of the shortcomings of academic education is its lack of attention to the component skills that are needed for effectiveness in a practical situation. But the opposite extreme of narrow specificity carries the danger that training and education become totally fragmented and lose all coherence. Educational technology holds great promise, but also some considerable peril: it encourages the trend toward the quick fix for the immediate need, the slick package for each distinct skill. If this is carried too far, corporate education could become an aggregate of a large number of separate and disconnected pieces that train "how" without teaching "why?"

Some corporations in fact pride themselves on their ability to analyze even complex functions in terms of specific component skills, and then to design training modules for each of these. One major insurance corporation, for example, identified 800 distinct competencies in the data-processing area, and is developing a self-contained module of instruction for each.

This can be wasteful and repetitious for the employer as well as for the individual employee. As change accelerates, and with it job content and necessary skills, it becomes ever more important to make learning cumulative so that overall understanding increases geometrically rather than linearly (Branscomb and Gilmore, 1975, p. 227). Separate skill elements must be grouped into more generic aptitudes, so that what has been learned before can be built upon and future learning needs can be anticipated as much as possible. Long-range cost-effectiveness can be enhanced by a measure of coherence and an overall pattern to the individual components of corporate programs. In this way, the whole can be made greater than the sum of the parts.

Furthermore, without a reasonable understanding of more general principles, individuals who know only which buttons to push in order to produce certain results are helpless in the face of breakdown or unanticipated events. The near disaster at Three Mile Island brought this to everyone's attention in a rather frightening manner. An extreme approach is equally inappropriate if one can be certain that the button and black boxes will soon be obsolete and make way for unpredictable new gadgetry and new processes. Employees would then essentially have to be retrained from scratch because so little underlying knowlege can be carried over from the previous training.

Clearly a balance needs to be struck between extreme task

specificity, and the academic tendency to start everything at the most basic theoretical level and to cram all remotely pertinent information into each course. There are severe limits on time, money, and energy that must be taken into consideration. One could easily envision a system of employee education so sweeping and so inclusive that everyone so trained knows and understands everything about the job and its context—but unfortunately has no time left to do the job. This is an issue that must be taken very seriously both in striking a balance as to the proper inclusion of underlying principles and also in deciding on the proper breadth of employee education. These questions are among the most important and most sensitive ones to be pursued jointly by employers and educators. They need to explore together, with regard to both professional preparation as well as the ongoing maintenance of skills, just what individuals need to know and to be able to do in order to be effective, and what priorities need to be set and choices made in deciding on programmatic content.

A third major issue needs to be raised with regard to the prevailing approach to employer-sponsored education. The growing impact of the social, economic, and political aspects of the business environment requires not only human and technical skills, but also a better understanding of the pertinent external circumstances. To date, the need for this has been reflected only to a limited extent in employee education. A few corporations include Washington-based programs as part of their executive development. The Brookings Institute, the American Enterprise Institute, and the U.S. Chamber of Commerce are among the organizations offering appropriate seminars and workshops of varying length and intensity. Some large corporations conduct their own programs in Washington, or in state capitals, using government officials, legislators, and other local experts as resources. Some of these activities are described in a recent Conference Board Report mentioned already in Chapter 5 (Lusterman, 1981). The report states that about one-third of the surveyed enterprises had during the preceding year provided for senior or middle managers some kind of activity dealing with "the political system and its methods: legislative, judicial and regulatory processes in the United States." About 7 percent of the companies provided some instruction regarding public-policy systems and processes in foreign countries where they operate (Lusterman, 1981, p. 24). However, a clear majority of the executives questioned find "important areas of neglect and underemphasis in current programs and approaches" (p. 33). Too few managers are involved and many of the pertinent activities are little more than an occasional lecture or discussion, usually focusing rather narrowly on the public-policy process.

In view of the widely held expectation that the environmental impact on managerial and professional activities will grow and that decision making will be increasingly decentralized, a more than superficial knowledge and understanding of the pertinent political, social, and economic factors should become a much more important component of employer-sponsored education. It should be included in programs for all supervisory, managerial, and professional levels, and should be both broadened and intensified beyond the current discussion of public-policy issues. The trend toward growing worker participation included in the QWL movement also suggests that some of these environmental factors should be included in developmental programs for the non-exempt work force.

Lustermann (1981, p. 6) summarizes the most important areas of needed competence:

- An "*awareness* that events in the business environment significantly affect company interests, and alertness to particular threats and opportunities."
- "*Sensitivity* to how company decisions will affect, and be perceived by, others."
- A change in the attitude that "business and government are in an inherently adversarial relationship."
- "Attentiveness to the opinions, values and interests of others."
- "Systematically monitoring and analyzing the business environment and integrating the data developed into strategic planning processes."

Reference has been made earlier to the growing chorus of criticism of contemporary management models in American industry. Hayes and Abernathy, Reich, Peters and Waterman, and others all call for a change from strict adherence to the traditional principles of scientific management. The suggested modifications and remedies differ in vocabulary and to some extent in substance. But through the writing of all the authors there is a common thread: they all call for a management style that uses a less hierarchical organization, provides more flexibility, and facilitates more personal initiative and participation at all levels. As Reich states, in his advocacy of what he calls a "flexible-system" model:

> Flexible systems can adapt quickly only if information is widely shared within them. There is no hierarchy to problem-solving; solutions may come from anyone, anywhere. In flexible-system enterprises, nearly everyone in the production process is responsible for recognizing problems and finding solutions. [1983, p. 135]

This book is concerned with issues of education and human development, not with management theories. But it is very clear that the changes in management that appear to be called for with such a degree of unanimity have profound educational implications. The degree of shared responsibility and participation desired by Reich, the "insight into the subtleties and complexities of strategic decisions" stressed by Hayes and Abernathy, the ability to "manage paradox and ambiguity" desired by Peters and Waterman—all of these call for a breadth of understanding that far exceeds what have traditionally been considered appropriate technical skills. Professional curricula will have to be considerably broadened if graduates are to be properly prepared to be effective in their jobs, and the additional components will have to be properly integrated to form a coherent whole rather than merely tacked on as "general education." But the environment continues to change, and breadth must therefore also be incorporated into ongoing employee education in order to maintain effectiveness on the job. Here, too, the task will be to provide this breadth as part of a coherent whole, rather than to maintain a dichotomy between human relations competence on the one hand, and technical skills on the other.

The tasks for educators and for employers, thus, are quite analogous. Tackling these difficult but important problems of arriving at the appropriate breadth in professional preparation as well as in continuing employee education cries out for close collaboration between business and universities. At this time, neither has the right answers. Each can learn greatly from the other.

The Need for a Longer-Range Perspective

The previous section suggested that there exists a point of diminishing return in making employee training too narrowly specific. It stressed the importance of moving toward a more coherent and cumulative approach, as one of the ways in which employers would benefit from a longer-range perspective with regard to their human resource requirements.

During the recent past, many businesses have made considerable progress in this regard. Function often follows form, so it is encouraging to note that throughout the corporate world, the label "human resources" has replaced "personnel." Many large enterprises now have vice presidents for human resource development. However, a 1982 study of top-management structure in 432 U.S. corporations indicates that these individuals are part of the senior management team in less than half of the companies (Shaeffer and Janger, 1982). Human resource considerations often are not included in corporate strategic planning. As a result, most employer-sponsored training is undertaken in reaction to changes that either have already taken place or are imminent. As described in Chapter 3, a large portion of such training is focused on bridge points in the employee's career: entry into the firm and lateral or vertical moves into new positions. Another substantial portion of employee development is designed to deal with changes in product, technology, regulation, or organization. All of this is more or less ad hoc, and with the exception of the successor-planning schemes of some large corporations, developmental needs are rarely anticipated well ahead of time.

Even in its most rudimentary form, more systematic planning of employee training on the part of employers would facilitate business-education cooperation and probably result in more carefully designed programs. Business and industry are quite justified in blaming colleges and universities for being excessively rigid and too slow in responding to external requests for programs. However, too many of these requests are unnecessarily last-minute. A longer-range perspective could in many cases result in more lead time and allow more joint planning and development of programs.

The need for the inclusion of human resource considerations in strategic planning, however, far transcends these operational considerations because of two very basic factors affecting the work-force requirements of business and industry. The first of these factors is the steady increase in the educational requirements of middle-level positions throughout both the manufacturing and the service sectors of our post-industrial society. The first chapter of this book discussed this issue at some length. The point was made there that the growing cost of preparing individuals for higher-level employment increasingly force both society in general and individual employers to view the skilled portion of the labor force as a substantial investment. It indeed constitutes *human capital,* a phrase that is much bandied about these days. Such investment must be protected, much as investment in bricks and mortar and in equipment must be protected. There is a need to plan for regular maintenance and renovation, scheduled as much in advance as possible during relatively slack periods. Last-minute decisions with regard to training are likely to be as disruptive and wasteful as emergency repairs. Furthermore, like physical plant and equipment, human capital can no longer be considered disposable. Even if an ample supply of new recruits were available at all times, a policy of always replacing the obsolescent individual with new employees would have unacceptable societal and human costs. This alone is reason enough to take a long-range view of employee development.

But a second major factor reinforces the need. The pool of new entrants into the labor force is not unlimited, and is about to shrink. Because of the aging products of the baby boom, society is about to face an unprecedented situation in which there will be, simultaneously, a population bulge in the middle years and a shortage of younger people. As those concerned with higher education know only too well, there are today already 20 percent fewer individuals under 18 than there were a decade ago. This trough now affects high schools and is about to impact on colleges. It would have already been felt by those enterprises that usually hire high school graduates were it not for the recent recession and high unemployment rate. Even so, there appears to be a serious shortage in some skilled trades such as mechanics and sheet-metal workers. In a few years, the post-bulge trough will have reached the mid-twenty age level (Masnick, 1982).

A recent report of the Bureau of Labor Statistics (Fullerton, 1982) shows that the growth of the labor force will fall from a high of 2.7 percent per year during the five-year period 1975–1979 to 1.3 percent in 1985–1900, and to less than 1 percent in 1990–1995. In absolute numbers, this means that the labor force during the last of these periods will grow by less than 6 million, whereas over 10 million workers were added between 1975 and 1980. Obviously, this has a substantial effect on the age distribution of the labor force.

In 1970, the 25–44-year-old segment of the population constituted 40 percent of the work force. It became 46 percent in 1980 and is projected to rise to over 54 percent by 1990 (Choate, 1982). As a result, as stated strikingly in a recent paper by Hodgkinson (1982): *"90 percent of the work force in 1990 is already at work today."* Hodgkinson points out that the situation will be further complicated by immigration and the differential fertility of different groups. As a result, minorities of all ages will constitute between 20 and 25 percent of the population by 1990, but their percentage among younger age groups will be over 30 percent. Given the current trend away from affirmative

action and toward more exclusionary college admissions practices, the changing composition of the youth cohort may well
result in a further decrease of the number of younger people
graduating from college or professional school during the coming years.

As a result, unless the economy is again in a deep recession
with a catastrophically high unemployment rate, there is likely
to be a severe shortage of college-trained individuals to fill the
traditional entry-level positions in the supervisory, managerial,
and professional occupations. If this is not anticipated well
ahead of time, one will again hear anguished outcries and
witness fierce competition for an inadequate number of
college graduates, much as has recently been the case with
regard to high-technology fields. There may in fact be a three-
way tug of war between employers wanting to meet immediate
needs, colleges wanting students for advanced training, and
the armed services waiting to fill their ranks. With reasonable
planning, however, by both employers and educators, alternatives can be identified and pursued at least to alleviate the im-
pending labor problem.

One such alternative is to bring about a fundamental
change in the attitude of employers toward their labor-force
needs. The prevalent view at this time continues to consider the
available pool of potential employees at all levels to be infinitely
elastic, with new hires always available to fill needs. This new-
hiring policy is also considered cheaper: new entrants com-
mand lower salaries, and they have acquired their up-to-date
skills at no expense to the employer. Little thought is given to
the developmental investment already made in someone who
has been with the company for some time. Such an individual
not only has acquired many of the necessary job-related skills
but has presumably become part of a team and has learned to
be sensitive to the specific needs and the special characteristics
of the firm. This represents an appreciable investment that is
often ignored. As a result, the general tendency is to rely
greatly on new appointments to meet new job requirements,
rather than to retrain the existing work force. Some experts
believe that current manpower shortages in the high-

technology industry could be alleviated if more of this were done: articles in *Fortune* (Main, 1982) and in the *Boston Globe* (Rosenberg, 1981) have suggested that in spite of the much-publicized need for more engineers in certain fields, companies devote few resources to retraining their own technical personnel who are in outmoded areas.

The consequences of demographic changes will create another serious challenge for employers. The majority of middle-age, middle-level employees are already beginning to find little or no room at the top (see, for example, Howard and Bray, 1980; Browne, 1983, p. 53). The upper levels of most organizations are filled with relatively young individuals who joined the staff at the beginning of the years of growth and prosperity. In the business world just as in the academy, these people at the top are nowhere near retirement. They clog the path for upward mobility for the many who are behind them, in the middle levels of the hierarchies. As a result, most businesses must address themselves to the educational as well as the emotional needs of those who will be staying at the plateau of these intermediate levels for perhaps twenty years or more. Their continuing effectiveness and vitality should be of paramount importance to their employers. Until now little attention has been paid to their developmental needs. The principal emphasis of employer-sponsored education has been on upward mobility, with programs geared to prepare individuals to climb from one level to the next. Not only content but also attitudes and value systems implicit in corporate education will have to change substantially. Rewards other than promotion will have to be devised. One possibility that has been raised is increased participation in decision making. This is consistent with some recent developments in organizational patterns such as matrix management, and is becoming much easier through computerized information systems with terminals at every desk. Obviously such broader involvement in decision making has substantial educational implications.

The conclusion of this section is clear. The growing cost of preparing individuals for most middle-level and many other positions, and the skewed age distribution of the work force during the coming decades combine to require a much longer-range view of human resource needs. Many enterprises, particularly a number of large corporations, have in recent years moved toward the norm of lifelong employment as a matter of policy. It may well become a matter of necessity for almost every employer. Viewing the work force as essentially stable and as constituting a long-range investment provides new opportunities for a systematic approach to education and training at all levels. But of course it creates problems as well, particularly for the small businesses. In a large corporation, there is more flexibility in the use of personnel, and if an individual leaves after having received a considerable amount of expensive training, this still constitutes only a small fraction of the total investment in human resource development. Not so for the smaller employer who may be seriously affected by such a loss of investment. This issue, which has broad policy implications, will be further discussed in the next chapter.

——————— CHAPTER 7 ———————

An Agenda for Joint Action

Coping with Accelerating Change

The average individual nearing retirement today went to college before the Second World War. It is something of an understatement to say that a lot has changed since then. The political and economic map of the world is quite different, and technology has been revolutionized first by the computer and then by the development of the microchip. Television is as common now as radio was then. Concepts like genetic engineering that had not even been thought about forty years ago are commonplace today. Changes in all aspects of society have been so numerous as to defy brief summary. As a result, much of the store of facts acquired before 1940 is obsolete or irrelevant today. Worse, many of the underlying ideas, basic concepts, and methodologies considered valid then are outdated today and have been replaced by quite different ones.

The societal changes of the past forty years have created many new categories of occupations and eliminated many others. Beyond that, however, these changes have fundamentally affected the content of virtually every job, particularly

129

those in the managerial and professional areas. To be a technician, an engineer, a middle-level manager, a health-care provider, a lawyer today requires substantially new information and also the understanding of new theories and methodologies that were not prevalent in 1940. And increasingly, keeping up with changes in one's job and maintaining one's effectiveness as a professional require more than on-the-job training or independent and self-directed reading of literature. Just as formal education has replaced apprenticeship in the preparation for most categories of higher occupation, so a need has emerged for repeated periods of organized instruction to keep up with changes. In response to this need, a substantial rise has taken place in recent years in the provision of various forms of continuing professional and other occupational education. As described in earlier chapters, much of this is being provided for employees by employers in both the public and the private sectors. Professional associations have become major providers of a wide variety of learning opportunities for their members. Last but certainly not least, the adult and continuing education activities of our colleges and universities have expanded a great deal.

Yet this has happened by and large in a reactive and ad hoc fashion, unsystematically and without a reexamination of several basic premises of our approach to education. The system as a whole continues to be predicated on the quite outdated notion that formal learning can be concentrated into the formative years of an individual and that the skills and perceptions then acquired will continue to be adequate for a lifetime of activity on the job and in society. The inadequacy of this view is being partially remedied by a patchwork of disconnected and scattered learning opportunities.

But these programs, with few exceptions, have remained on the periphery of our educational institutions, largely ignored or even disdained by the faculty. In most institutions of higher education a sharp distinction remains between continuing education and the traditional programs intended for and taken by the younger students. These programs, in turn, still reflect only past change. They are in general up to date in terms of content, but are designed and delivered as if they were terminal programs, rather than the first stage of a continuing and recurrent process of learning. The basic premise shaping most of higher education today continues to be that it is possible to learn first and to do later, and that the principal instructional task of the college or university is accomplished when the individual graduates.

This cannot continue. The long-range perspective advocated in Chapter 6 for employers must also be acquired by educators. Their obligation to do so is even greater because by its very nature the educational system is society's principal mechanism for coping not just with the present but also with the future. And the most cursory look ahead indicates very clearly that the pace of change prevalent during recent decades will continue and probably even accelerate. The time scale of technological evolution, once measured in centuries and then in decades, continues to shrink to a point at which a span of a few years can bring about developments that affect a wide number of occupations in quite basic ways. Add to this the considerations mentioned in the previous chapter that force us to view the skilled work force not as a disposable and transient element that can be hired and fired at will, but as a stable human resource representing a considerable investment. The conclusion becomes evident: our society's educators, employers, and policy makers must readjust their thinking and must recognize that *educational development for the advanced occupations is a recurrent and lifelong process.*

It is important to emphasize that this introduces a new element into the discussion of adult and continuing education. The past twenty years have witnessed substantial progress toward greater opportunities for the adult learner. There is widespread recognition of the great need to provide a belated opportunity to enter or to complete higher education programs for many indivduals who were unable to do so when they were young. External degree programs, assessment of prior experience, credit by examination, and many other innovations have provided access to many for whom full-time study after high school was impossible. At the same time, the vastly expanded system of adult and continuing education also reflects the increasing likelihood that individuals may wish or be forced to make one or more career changes (Aslanian and Brickell, 1980) and also that growing life expectancy and changing working conditions increase the demand for self-fulfilling leisure activities. All in all, much is being done and much has been written about meeting the needs of adults for lateral and upward mobility and for enrichment. By now, these can be viewed as the "traditional" purposes of adult education.

The gap that this view leaves is an important one: it neglects the growing role of recurrent education as essential for *job maintenance*. A variety of opportunities for formal education is needed not only to climb up or sideways on the grid of occupations, but increasingly also *just to stay in place.* Accelerating societal change makes of each job a treadmill on which the individual must move rapidly to remain up to date and effective. The *maintenance of occupational effectiveness* is emerging as a major, indeed perhaps the most important, reason for the availability of lifelong educational opportunities. We need a new concept: *occupational maintenance.* (Lynton, 1983a,b)

To date, this concept has received attention primarily in the licensed professions (Houle, 1980; Phillips, 1983; Berry and Roederer, 1983). A substantial number of states have instituted relicensure or recertification for a variety of occupations ranging from accounting to veterinary medicine. In many cases, continued practice has been made conditional on mandatory continuing education. The effectiveness of existing licensure and relicensure procedures is a matter of considerable debate and growing doubt, with some aspects being tested in court. Many questions are also being raised about the prevailing tendency to formulate continuing education requirements in purely quantitative terms—so many hours—without any measure either of quality or of impact on the competence of the practititioner. But no one questions the basic premise that it is as important to ensure the maintenance of the skills and the effectiveness of licensed professionals as it is to require high standards of competence as a condition for the initial authorization to practice.

The need for maintenance of effectiveness is just as great in the many occupations and professions that are not regulated and licensed by the state. Realization of this is gradually emerging from various quarters. A substantial contribution to defining the issues and to raising widespread awareness was made by a recent report published under the auspices of the Department of Electrical and Computer Engineering at MIT (Bruce et al., 1982). The report, entitled "Lifelong Cooperative Education," addresses itself primarily to engineering, which is a field in which both the accelerating rate of change and the limited pool of available human resources are particularly obvious. But the basic points made with regard to engineering are applicable to most other occupations that require advanced skills and higher education. The following excerpt from the MIT report applies therefore to many fields other than engineering:

> The future vitality and competitiveness of U.S. high technology industry depend on widespread acceptance of lifelong formal educational activities as integral components of productive engineering work. This is so because:
>
> - The present rapid rate of scientific and technical innovation invalidates one of the basic assumptions underlying the traditional structure of engineering education: that a few years of formal education can provide an adequate foundation for a lifetime of professional engineering work.
> - The demand for highly creative, up-to-date engineers has intensified during the last decade as a result of the rapid growth of the knowledge-intensive industry and of the increasing competition for national and international markets.
> - This demand cannot be met by replacing "obsolescent" engineers with new graduates (and the human costs of such a replacement policy would be unacceptable even if it were feasible).

- The only apparent alternative is better utilization of the presently available engineering workforce through continuing education at the work place, with the active encouragement and support of employers. (Bruce et al., p. 6)

The implications of this are significant enough to call not merely for a substantial increase in the quantity of continuing education, but also for some very fundamental changes in content. The following paragraphs will examine occupational maintenance (shortened to OM) in greater detail.

Lifelong Occupational Maintenance

The immediately obvious characteristic of OM is that it really should constitute "continuing" education: it should be a continuation of the preparatory formative phase. All parts together should be viewed as a single, lifelong process of development, as a long chain with longer and shorter links. One of these may precede employment—but there is already a trend in some schools of business to require at least two years of practical experience before admission into an MBA program. Subsequent links are likely to be provided in various places by a variety of sources: institutions of higher education, employers, the training industry, professional associations, and perhaps others.

This raises, as a first issue for exploration and discussion, the question of the extent to which it is desirable and feasible to establish coherence and continuity for this multifaceted lifelong process. At one extreme there is the status quo, which ignores any relationship among successive phases of OM. For all the reasons already mentioned, this extreme results in duplication of effort and a waste of time and resources for both the individual and the employer. At the other extreme is a vision —attractive to the orderly mind—of a highly continuous and cumulative process each phase of which is based on preceding ones and anticipates those that will follow. It is likely that the achievement of such a utopian goal will require too high a degree of coordination and regulation to make it feasible. Some intermediate approach needs to be developed. Virtually no thought has been given until now to this issue by any of the pertinent constituencies, but consideration of the problem should be a matter of high priority for the educational establishment, for public and private employers, and for policy makers.

A second fundamental question is somewhat easier to define and to tackle. What would be the implications about content, length, and timing of the first link of the recurrent chain of education if OM were to be ensured by public policies and private actions? If one could be reasonably certain that every manager, engineer, physician, technician, and all others in middle- and higher-level positions would participate in an appropriate amount of OM, how would the curriculum leading to the first professional degree be revised? If OM would supply both fine tuning of specialized skills and continuous updating of broader, contextual knowledge, could the initial educational phase be shorter? Should it be less specialized? If so, does this mean more emphasis on theoretical principles, or more broadening into cognate and environmental topics? Again, this is an issue that has barely been broached to date, and to which much attention needs to be devoted by higher education in close collaboration with employers.

This collaboration is central to the proper development of OM. The concept that professional development is a lifelong process inevitably means that, again quoting the MIT report, it is essential to replace "the present discontinuity between full-time study and full-time work by a gradual transition extending through most of . . . professional life." There needs to be "Intermixing of work, study and teaching with the active support of employers . . . [and] close collaboration between faculties and their industrial colleagues, amounting to a joint membership in an 'extended academic community'" (Bruce 1982, p. 32).

It is important to note that the vision of Fano and his colleagues goes well beyond collaboration between education and industry in designing and providing OM. Not only in engineering but also in other rapidly changing fields, the latest techniques and the newest equipment are more likely to be found in the corporate than in the academic world. This is obvious when it comes to the latest generation of computers or the most advanced methods in genetic engineering. But it is also true in fields such as accounting and financial management. Hence, institutions of higher education stand to benefit greatly from a reverse transfer of knowledge. At the same time, business, industry, and government increasingly need direct contact with faculty for consultation, policy analysis, and technical assistance because of the growing complexity and interconnectedness of information in the contemporary knowledge explosion. It becomes increasingly important to have faculty involved in synthesizing and interpreting fragments of information into usable and directly applicable knowledge (*Cf.*, e.g., O'Keefe, 1983; Lynton, 1983c; Lindblom and Cohen, 1979).

All of this calls for a two-way flow of information and ideas between the work place and the academy as an essential element of OM and to benefit both sides. Furthermore, the inevitable shortages of physical and human resources that will arise periodically in certain fields will require the joint use of individuals as well as facilities. This will be discussed further in the next chapter.

Overarching this variety of educational and operational implications of OM are a number of important and difficult policy issues that urgently require the attention of higher education, business and industry, and government (O'Keefe, 1977). Foremost among these issues is the perennial question: *Who pays?*

The financing of adult and continuing education has received much attention in recent years, particularly in Europe, but also by a number of observers in this country. Most of these are described in recent books edited by Anderson (1982), Kuhlenkamp and Schütze (1982), and Levin and Schütze (1983). The wide range of approaches described in these volumes reflects in part that there really are three fairly distinct categories of adult education.

The first of these is the one that has received the most attention in this country and has already been described at the beginning of this chapter. It consists of those educational opportunities for the adult learner aimed primarily at enrichment and personal advancement. The individual participant is the principal beneficiary, and therefore this category of continuing education is usually expected to be self-supporting through tuition and fees. Payment or reimbursement of these costs has come increasingly to be recognized as an important condition of work and is now included in many collective-bargaining agreements and in the contracts of many exempt employees (Wirtz, 1979; Barton, 1982). In Europe, more emphasis has been placed on paid educational leave.

There are also those who argue that the societal benefits of an optimally educated citizenry warrant public support of such individually oriented continuing education. The references cited above contain both American and European proposals for government-financed mechanisms such as individual educational entitlements and vouchers to allow everyone to pursue their education at will.

Public benefit and therefore public financing of continuing education are even more appropriate for that category of adult education aimed primarily at preventing or reducing unemployment and generally, to mitigate against substantial labor-market dislocations. The changing nature of the work force described in Chapter 1 has led to the growing realization that job programs cannot have much impact unless they contain a substantial educational component. A number of labor economists and others have argued that the expenditures for appropriate educational opportunities may well be smaller than expenditures for unemployment compensation and the related social costs of unemployment. One of the most striking proposals within this context is that of the Dutch labor expert, Emmerij, (1983) who suggests a program of paid educational sabbaticals for all workers as a cost-effective way of spreading job opportunities and avoiding unemployment.

Both of these categories of continuing education fall primarily within the general framework of social policy. By contrast, recurrent education to maintain occupational effectiveness must be viewed as part of economic policy because it serves to preserve the investment in human capital required for

the maintenance of productivity. It follows that the benefi-
ciaries of this type of continuing education are not only the individual participants and society at large, but also the employers. OM provides the systematic maintenance and renovation
of human capital. For this reason, it is as important to the employer as regular maintenance and overhaul of buildings and
equipment. The MIT group uses characteristic engineering
language to state that in the case of equipment, "the necessary
equipment downtime is routinely scheduled and accepted by all
parties." In the same way, they argue, "downtime" for continuing education needs to be accepted as an essential part of the
working pattern of engineers (Bruce et al., 1982, p. 20).

Clearly, then, employers are a key constituency of OM.
They must be directly involved and derive direct benefits, and
should also bear much of the cost. However, this does not obvi-
ate the desirability of incentives provided through direct or indirect public subsidies. This happens, after all, in the case of
buildings and equipment. The government recognizes that investment in the maintenance and renovation of industry's physical infrastructure is important to the economy generally. For
this reason, such activity is state supported in a variety of ways,
through tax incentives, or offsets, accelerated depreciation, and
at times, by direct subsidies. By the same token, therefore, one
ought to consider the role of national, state, and local government in the financing of OM as important as that of employers
and individuals.

A full discussion of the complex issue of public support for
OM goes beyond the purview of this book; two details, however, are nevertheless worth emphasizing. First, the widespread
implementation of a system of OM requires more than one-on-
one contracts between employers and providers. It also
requires a considerable infrastructure with a number of components: the development of performance standards as well as
instruments for assessment of instructional needs, and a
network of information about available programs as well as
mechanisms to develop long-range human resource projections
(Lynton, 1983b). A considerable amount of thought and attention should be given to the nature of these building blocks for

an OM infrastructure, and it is hoped that this will begin to happen in the near future. Even in the absence of such work, however, one can take the position that public support for OM should concentrate primarily on the development of these components. No one employer or employee organization will do so.

A second point about public support for OM can be made as well. As mentioned earlier, all available information about employer-sponsored education indicates that small enterprises provide relatively little of this for their staff. One of the principal reasons is the understandable fear that an employee, once brought up to date at the expense of the company, will change jobs and this expenditure will benefit another employer. A large corporation may be able to afford this, especially since they can fairly assume that they will gain as much as they lose on the average through such employee movements. In addition, more and more larger enterprises are moving toward policies of lifelong employment. But the small company cannot do this, and cannot afford to train its employees for the benefit of competitors.

This issue can be at least partially resolved through a system whereby all employers bear an equivalent financial burden for employee education. One way of bringing this about is to levy a tax on all private-sector employers based either on the number of employees and/or on the magnitude of the payroll. The revenues generated could be used for direct support of OM infrastructure and programs. To the extent to which employers organize and fund their own programs, their tax contribution can be offset by the amount of their own expenditures. This is essentially the system used in France, where in 1971 a law was passed regarding *formation continue,* which imposes a payroll tax currently at 1.9 percent. Direct company expenditures for employee education are subtracted from that. Peterson et al. (1982) describe the French system as well as the laws regarding worker education in other countries, and furnish an extensive bibliography.

Opinions about the effectiveness of the French system vary, as they do about other approaches, and no specific recommendation on this issue is being made here. The point that is being made is that in the exploration of appropriate funding policies for OM, serious consideration needs to be given to the development of approaches that will encourage maximum participation by the small business sector which employs a considerable proportion of the total work force.

The issue of benefit is closely related to that of responsibility. Which segment of society bears the principal responsibility for ensuring that the occupational effectiveness of our national work force is maintained by an appropriate system of recurrent education? Is it the state, be it at the national or the local level? Or is this the task of the employers, the individual, or the educational establishment? And how is this responsibility to be carried out: enforcement by regulation or encouragement by incentives?

In a number of professions where state licensure or certification is required, many states have chosen the former of these two alternatives. They require periodic relicensure or recertification for which a certain quantity of recurrent professional education is a prerequisite (Phillips, 1983). By contrast, in the teaching profession, which is also a state-certified field, recurrent professional education is widely encouraged by providing incentives: salary and/or rank increases are often based on continuing education credit.

This in turn raises questions about the extent to which OM should incorporate credits and credentials, whether in the form of degrees or of certificates. A decision to move in this direction would intensify the need for widespread coordination in order to ensure comparability and portability of the credential.

The purpose of this discussion is to focus on the need for OM and to draw attention to the range of basic policy issues that need to be addressed in order to develop a viable and acceptable system. Recent months have witnessed an upsurge of interest in human resource development and its relationship to economic vitality. To date, the principal focus has been on the preparatory phase of education, which is indeed of great importance. But for all the reasons mentioned earlier, it is not enough to provide even the most excellent training prior to employment; the acceleration of change in our society requires that equal attention be paid to the maintenance of occupational effectiveness. There is great need to develop, at long last, a coherent and effective national policy with regard to manpower and education (Carnevale, 1982; Hoy, 1982; Choate, 1982; Carnevale and Goldstein, 1983) that recognizes that *maintenance* of human capital is as important as its initial development.

Maximizing Flexibility

Miracles rarely happen, and it is unlikely—indeed, perhaps it is not even desirable—that a national manpower and education policy will suddenly emerge, like Venus from some celestial shell, fully formed and perfect. At best, we can expect the more likely scenario according to which some first steps are taken that might provide a foundation on which further elements of a comprehensive policy can be developed.

The process of development is one which, of necessity, must be both collaborative and ongoing. It must involve all pertinent constituencies: educators, employers, unions and professional associations, and appropriate government agencies. Furthermore, it must take place simultaneously not only at the national level but also locally and regionally. There are many regional demographic differences in the availability of educational resources and in concentration of employment. Certain aspects of human resource development and maintenance may therefore call for different approaches in different parts of the country. Other issues are likely to transcend regional differences and require national attention.

It is therefore important to establish cooperative mechanisms both locally and nationally with the responsibility of devising an optimal approach to human resource issues. Two fundamental tasks must be tackled. The first is to identify the policy issues related to human capital development and maintenance, such as those suggested in the previous chapter, and to pursue appropriate legislative or other action for the resolution of these issues. Part of this task would also be to monitor the effectiveness of the approaches being tried, and to suggest modifications as necessary.

A second major task is to undertake, in an ongoing and continuously self-correcting fashion, the best possible projection of future manpower needs. It is very important that this go beyond a mere estimate of the number of individuals needed in various areas of specialization. This kind of planning is currently being done in an increasingly sophisticated manner by the U.S. Bureau of Labor Statistics and is being updated regularly on the basis of changing economic forecasts and other factors. These quantitative projections, however, are not sufficient. They need to be accompanied, as well, by estimates of changes in the *content* of various occupations. Educational demands are generated not only by changes in the necessary numbers of engineers or nurses or office workers, but also by changes in the skills needed in these occupations. Much too little has been devoted to this until now, and many apparent shortages of skilled labor could have been avoided if changing skill requirements had been anticipated earlier and more systematically. In order to achieve reasonable accuracy in projecting human resource needs, it is as imperative to pay attention to evolving job content as it is to consider shifts in the numbers of each occupation.

Even under the best of circumstances, however, forecasts are subject to substantial uncertainty. With continuing and accelerating societal change, there are bound to be unexpected fluctuations in demand. Some of these may be due to sudden crises, political or economic; others may arise because of quite unanticipated innovations. Whatever the cause, we can be certain only of uncertainty, and the overarching agenda item for cooperation between employers, educators, and government is therefore the achievement of optimal flexibility of human resource development and maintenance. This has a number of components that need to be explored and elaborated in a joint effort between business, education, and other constituencies. There must be a true meeting of the minds as to the best approaches, with agreement on quite specific steps, rather than in terms of glittering and quite meaningless generalities. Furthermore, the agreement must be reached and promulgated at the higher levels of the institutions involved and then implemented at the operational level. It is not enough to make pious statements at the top that are then ignored in practice.

The first component of flexibility in human resource development is breadth. The inevitability of the unexpected reinforces the need to strike a proper balance between general understanding and specific skills, in both preparatory and on-the-job education. At every stage there is a need both to prepare for the specific needs of the moment and to provide a degree of adaptability to the changing demands of tomorrow. At this time, neither higher education nor the business world takes the correct approach. Academic programs are too general and too abstract. They fail to prepare adequately for short-term utilization of knowledge and it is not clear that they really provide the proper foundation for continuing readjustment. At the same time, it is very much in the interest of the employer to lessen the degree of specificity and to broaden the content of employee education to make it more cumulative and to enhance the ability to deal with unexpected changes.

The issue of breadth is an excellent example of the need for substantive and quite detailed discussions between employers, educators, and others as to what can and should really be done. Few topics are more subject to the use of empty rhetoric. Both business and educational leaders often extol the benefits of a liberal education, but in practice, curricula remain narrowly specialized, albeit in a highly abstract fashion, and recruiters still give preference to graduates with professional degrees. This situation will persist if there is not more systematic discussion involving both executive and working levels on both sides.

Arriving at a mutually acceptable balance between breadth and specialization will be easier if it is coupled with the development of a coherent approach to a lifelong and recurrent pattern of education, as discussed in the previous chapter. Repeated periods of education during employment can be used for the fine tuning and deepening of skills. If everyone can count on this, there will be more willingness to accept greater breadth in the preparatory phase. In addition, it will also be possible to discuss a *shortening of the pipeline.* This would be a second major contribution to increasing the flexibility of human resource development. A major problem today is due to the pipeline effect: with four, five, or even more years in higher education required for the first professional degree, it takes that long to adjust in a significant manner to changing external demands. The current push to increase enrollment in engineering schools, for example, will result only a few years hence in a larger number of graduates. That does little to alleviate current shortages—and it has happened in the past that by the time the increased number of graduates emerge, needs have again changed. There is no way to eliminate this time lag entirely, but cutting back the initial educational period would be very helpful. This could be done if indeed a recurrent pattern of continuing education were ensured. It would blur the distinction between pre-employment education and the further stages of development that every individual would require. Educators, employers, and others would increasingly recognize that the process is a continuous one in which each stage builds on the previous one and provides a new measure of adaptation to current needs.

Shortening the pipeline and at the same time widening it by decreasing the degree of specialization will enhance the adaptability of higher education to fluctuating resource needs through new entrants into the labor market. But, as mentioned before, there are demographic, economic, and psychological reasons to pay more attention, as well, to the more effective use of those who are already employed. An essential element of the joint planning by employers and educators is to develop a shared strategy with regard to *optimal deployment of all available human resources.* As certain needs arise and others develop in an unexpected fashion, there will exist at any given time a certain aggregate of unmet occupational skills. These can be provided in two ways: by appropriate development of new recruits, and by retraining and updating of individuals in outmoded or less necessary areas. There can be no fixed and rigid prescription for this in individual cases. But much can be gained from a broad look undertaken jointly by all the pertinent constituencies. This could result in general guidelines that suggest the optimal allocation of resources and the best developmental strategy. To cite again the example of engineers and computer science, it would be very useful at this time to look both nationally and locally at the best way to meet these shortages. How many individuals in cognate areas are available who could be redirected with a limited amount of additional education to meet urgent needs? What is the best mix between allocating resources to this kind of retraining and providing funds for the initial training of new scientists and engineers?

This category of questions cannot be approached without taking due consideration of the wide variety of existing mechanisms for training and education. We have discussed several major components: the traditional system of educational institutions, corporate in-house programs, and the training industry. Any cooperative and systematic approach to human resource development must also consider the optimal division of responsibility among these quite different providers. The overall task is far too great for any one component of the disaggregated development system, and there is little justification for unnecessary duplication and blind competition. Instead it is appropriate to explore which aspect of human resource development can best be undertaken by which component of the system. What can colleges and universities do best? What is the optimal responsibility of the secondary, the vocational, the community college sector? What can business and industry best do in house and what can they most advantageously obtain from third-party vendors?

Again, the need is not for a prescriptive blueprint, but rather for an ongoing broad-brush assessment that provides a number of useful guidelines to policy and decision makers in all sectors. Each individual institution, employer, and employee will continue to meet the needs of the moment in whatever way appears to be the most advantageous and effective. But in making the choices among a complex set of alternatives, all concerned would be helped by being able to look beyond the surrounding tangle of trees. An overview of the forest is likely to become increasingly useful.

In considering that portion of the forest provided by cooperation between employees and educators, greater flexibility in human resource development can also be achieved by blurring the distinction between faculty and non-academic professionals. *Joint use of individuals* is becoming increasingly important. The MIT "Report on Lifelong Cooperative Education" points out the need for an "extended academic community" bridging the work place and the classroom in order to achieve the necessary reciprocal flow of knowledge and adaptation of attitudes (Bruce et al., 1982, pp. 32–33).

But more will be necessary. There is no way, with the best possible planning and optimal flexibility, that academic institutions will be able to keep pace with manpower demands in the light of inevitable surprises. Time and again there will be an unanticipated need, either in kind or in scope, to which a college or a university cannot completely adjust by using only its own faculty or its own facilities. There already exists an acute shortage of qualified faculty in computer science and other high-technology areas, and no scheme of increased salaries and other incentives can change that. Business and higher education will have to work out systematic ways of using corporate professionals on a part-time basis to augment instructional resources. This cannot be left to individual initiative but must be institutionalized through discussions and planning at the highest level.

The same is true of another important step in achieving ongoing adaptability to unexpected and often temporary needs: *shared use of facilities and equipment.* Colleges and universitiees are not likely to keep up with state-of-the-art instrumentation in rapidly changing fields of science and technology, and in addition, physical facilities are not easily or quickly adaptable to changing teaching patterns. Much can be gained by systematic and ongoing exploration of using these material resources for multiple purposes.

Having explored a number of areas that require the close collaboration of business, education, government, unions, and professional associations, one needs to ask: what forum will be able to provide these functions? What mechanism can bring about joint exploration and ongoing collaboration with regard to human resource development? The answer is not an easy one, but one can outline some possibilities. In the first place, it is clear that extremes must be avoided. On the one hand, it is not enough to establish at either the local or the national level some kind of advisory group representing all pertinent constituencies and meeting perhaps once or twice a year. By and large, such undertakings waste everyone's time because they can do little more than issue pronouncements of useless generality. The issues are too complex and indeed too subtle for an approach like that.

At the other extreme, one also needs to shun the establishment of yet another substantial bureaucratic apparatus, with a large staff producing volumnious and unread reports. There exist, at both the national and the state and/or regional levels, a variety of mechanisms responsible for the collection and analysis of pertinent data. The Census Bureau, the Bureau of Labor Statistics, the National Center for Educational Statistics, the Conference Board, and several professional associations are just a few among many from whom a very large amount of highly relevant and useful information can be garnered.

An appropriate middle ground may be provided if states were to establish *Human Resource Councils.* These should consist of influential chief executives from education, business, labor, and government, appointed by the governors in ways that shield the groups as much as possible from having a political cast and give them the maximum visibility and prestige. Each council would require a small but very capable staff that would identify, assemble, and analyze the information and data bases required to development multiyear projections of changes in human resource needs for the state. These projections would be based on a combination of the following:

- increases as well as decreases in the number of jobs in different occupational categories;
- anticipated retirements and other factors creating job vacancies;
- changes in job content requiring new skills;
- demographic developments;

- estimates of underutilized human resources, including number of displaced workers, as well as non-traditional entrants into the work force such as housewives and the elderly seeking part-time employment.

Most of the pertinent information is available from secondary sources. After the initial effort of gathering this material, regular updating will not require a large staff.

On the basis of these data and with the help of the staff, each Human Resource Council should periodically assess the following for its state:

- the anticipated overall needs for human resource development and maintenance through education and training;
- the optimal strategy to meet the totality of these needs by combining the retraining of existing employees as well as displaced workers, with the initial training and education of the traditional younger cohort as well as the non-traditional entrants into the work force;
- the best way of combining the resources of educational institutions, employee-sponsored in-house programs, and the resources of third-party vendors in order to meet the overall developmental needs.

These assessments might be issued in the format of annual reports by the council on the *State of Human Resources.* These would serve as guidelines for public as well as private actions in the area of education and training. Without being coercive or constituting a rigid blueprint, the reports and recommendations of the council could be used to inform the allocation of resources at every level. Governors and legislatures could use them both during their deliberations on the budgetary support of education and also in considering tax incentives and other policies for other forms of human resource development. Private enterprises would find them helpful in decisions regarding their own plans for employee development. And educational institutions as well as private vendors would be assisted in their choices as to the nature and extent of the programs each should emphasize.

In addition, each Human Resource Council should analyze

pertinent state and local policies and make recommendations as appropriate. An analogous activity should be undertaken at the national level, with presidential appointments. A national Human Resource Council would of course use aggregate information and data and focus on countrywide trends, requirements, and policies.

Such a network of councils could be developed without elaborate legislation or substantial operating funds. It is likely to have benefits quite out of proportion to its costs, because it would create, for the first time, an adequate system of human resource information, which is essential to any kind of planning. Employers could use it to anticipate needs and to strike a realistic balance between relying on new employees and retraining current ones. Educational institutions and state coordinating agencies will be able to make more informed decisions about program development and resource allocations. Individuals will have more data to guide their career choices. And with such an information system, all constituencies can move toward a strategy of preventive maintenance of that scarce resource —human capital.

CHAPTER 8

Concluding Remarks: A New Model for the University

THE PRECEDING CHAPTERS have described a number of practical steps that can be taken by higher education and employers to enhance the connection between the two sectors. The obvious underlying premise, discussed repeatedly throughout the book, is that strengthening the connection is likely to benefit both sides.

However, there is an overarching theme that transcends the issue of university-business cooperation in employee education, the theme that educators and employers share a common interest in the development and maintenance of society's human resources. In one sense this is a truism that has always been valid, but changing societal conditions, the acceleration of change, and the ever-increasing need for knowledge and information have brought about fundamental changes in the way in which this common interest must be manifested and implemented. In an earlier age, the role and interests of education and employment were sequential: their respective domains touched each other at quite clearly defined interfaces. Learning

151

came first, and then work, and there was only a limited need for communication and cooperation across that temporal boundary.

But now the two have become inextricably intertwined. Both the number and kinds of jobs available and the content of these jobs is changing at an increasing rate. Theory and practice must be interrelated more and more closely. Education and employment must be woven together into a complex web requiring a degree of collaboration quite unlike anything in the past. New knowledge must be interpreted, disseminated, and applied much more directly and rapidly than in the past. The development of the necessary relationships calls for much more than a number of operational adjustments. It will require fundamental attitudinal changes on the part of those who make public policy, as well of employers and educators.

Carnevale (1982), Choate (1982), and Hoy (1982) are three voices in the growing chorus of individuals who recently have pointed out the need for a systematic human-capital policy on state, regional, and national levels. Employers and policymakers must learn to view the work force as an essential resource that is sharply limited in its quantity, not every elastic in it sresponse to changing demands, and requires systematic long-range plans for optimal maintenance. Strategic planning has been a corporate buzz word for many years, and industrial policy is rapidly becoming a major political issue. Both terms mean different things to different people, but in all their possible interpretations both require the inclusion of a human resource component directed at systematic preparation of new entrants into the work force, at retraining those displaced through labor market shifts, and at updating and renewing the skills and competencies of those facing changing job content.

The inclusion of human resource consideration in public and private strategies for economic development will require substantial changes in the prevailing attitude that the labor market is unlimited and highly elastic. But such changes will not profoundly affect the basic nature of the institutions of government or of the corporate sector. For higher education, on the other hand, the implications of the necessary changes are much more profound. The traditional model for academic institutions, particularly for universities, is characterized by considerable isolation from the outside world. Both in time and in location the institutional boundaries are clearly defined. The full-time resident student is the norm, as is the emphasis on basic research for its own sake and on communicating its results primarily to fellow scholars. The model is further characterized by sharp internal boundaries: between the liberal arts and the professional subjects, between regular instruction and continuing education, between credit and noncredit programs, and between matriculated and special students.

The relationships between higher education and its external constituencies suggested in this book will require profound changes in this model. They will result in an institution no longer isolated but indeed so closely intertwined with society as to no longer have clear boundaries in time, in location, or even in membership. The MIT Report (Bruce et al., 1982) calls for an "extended academic community" with much movement of individuals between campus and workplace, both as students and as instructors. Cooperation has to extend to a dialogue about program needs and program content. There is even a need for a real sharing of authority in matters long considered the inviolable prerogative of the faculty. In addition, the growing need for the interpretation of knowledge and for its more rapid dissemination and application requires more faculty involvement in applied research, technical assistance, and public information. In turn, this implies a substantial change in the internal value and reward system of universities.

These are not easy changes, and they are not without danger. Some observers have expressed the fear that too much adaptation to external needs would lead to a degree of co-optation and subservience certain to destroy the cherished autonomy of higher education. Others warn that too much stress on applied scholarship will weaken the universities' attention to fundamental and nondirected research. These are indeed crucial issues. A civilized and democratic society requires a strong and independent academy as its principal source of disinterested critique and as its locus for the pursuit of knowledge for its own sake. There is no question that every effort must be made to maintain academic detachment and integrity, as well its long-range perspective.However, we can no longer do so by means of isolation. That is the way in which academic institutions have safeguarded their independence in the past, but isolation is a luxury that neither the academy nor society can any longer afford. The growth of higher education and the economy's dependence on highly skilled human resources, as well as on effective technology transfer, has rendered the ivory tower obsolete. As President Derek Bok of Harvard has stated:

> The cloistered university could probably exist only at a heavy cost to the quality of professional education, applied research, social criticism and expert advice—activities that are all important to our society. (Bok, 1982, p. 73)

It is interesting that Bok includes social criticism as requiring a tearing down of the cloister walls. That is the paradox that must be faced: the most vital function of the academy requires both involvement and detachment. It can no longer remain aloof, yet it cannot lose its identity and become merely another piece in the societal mosaic. Striking the balance between isolation and assimilation is the great challenge to be faced if higher education is to survive as a force in postindustrial society. There is a need to develop a new model for the university of the future, one that retains its timeless objectives to create and to disseminate knowledge but which does so by new means appropriate to new circumstances. That subject will be pursued elsewhere.

Bibliography

ABELSON, PHILIP, "Lessons from Medical School," *Science*, 215, p. 1461, 1982.

ABERNATHY, W. J., KIM CLARK AND ALAN KANTROW, *Industrial Renaissance*, New York, Basic Books, 1983.

ADKINS, DOUGLAS L., "The American Educated Labor Force: An Empirical Look at Theories of Its Formation and Composition," *Higher Education and the Labor Market*, ed. Margaret S. Gordon, New York, McGraw-Hill, 1974.

ALFORD, HAROLD J., ed., *Power and Conflict in Continuing Education*, Belmont, CA, Wadsworth, 1980.

AMA Directory of Management Education Programs, New York, American Management Associations, 1978.

AMERICAN SOCIETY FOR TRAINING AND DEVELOPMENT, "ASTD National Report," Washington, D.C., June 26, 1980.

ANDERSON, RICHARD E., ed., *The Cost and Financing of Adult Education*, New York, Lexington Books, 1982.

ANDERSON, RICHARD E., "Problems of Collecting Financial Data for Adult Education and Training," *Proceedings of the ASTD National Issues Forum*, Washington, D.C., Am. Soc. Training Dev., 1983.

ARGYRIS, CHRIS, AND DONALD A. SCHÖN, *Theory in Practice: Increasing Professional Effectiveness*, San Francisco, Jossey-Bass, 1974.

ASLANIAN, CAROL B., AND HENRY M. BRICKELL, *Americans in Transition*, New York, College Entrance Examination Board, 1980.

155

BAKER, JEANNETTE S., "An Analysis of Degree Programs Offered by Selected Industrial Corporations," Univ. of Arizona (unpublished), 1983.

BARONE, MICHAEL, "Too Professional," *The Washington Post,* May 19, 1983.

BARTON, PAUL E., *Worklife Transitions,* New York, McGraw-Hill, 1982.

BEAL, DENTON, ed., *The American Education Deskbook,* Washington, D.C., Editorial Projects in Education, 1982.

BECKER, GARY S., "Underinvestment in College Education," *Am. Economic Review* (Supplement), May 1960, pp. 346–354.

BECKER, GARY S., *Human Capital: A Theoretical and Empirical Analysis, with Special Reference to Education,* New York, Columbia University Press, 1964.

BECKER, GARY S., *Human Capital: A Theoretical and Empirical Analysis, with Special Reference to Education,* 2nd edition, Chicago, University of Chicago Press, 1974.

BELL, DANIEL, *The Reforming of General Education: The Columbia College Experience in Its National Setting,* New York, Columbia University Press, 1966.

BELL, DANIEL, *The Coming of Post-Industrial Society,* New York, Basic Books, 1973.

BERG, IVAN, *Education and Jobs: The Great Training Robbery,* New York, Praeger, 1970.

BERRY FRANCES STOKES, AND DOUG ROEDERER, "State Regulation of Occupations and Professions" in *The Book of the State,* Lexington, KY, The Council of State Governments, 1983.

BIRD, C., *The Case Against College,* New York, McKay, 1975.

BLAIR, WILLIAM G., "Scientific Detail Overwhelms Regard for Human Needs at Medical Schools," *The New York Times* (II), p. 3, Oct. 21, 1982.

BLOUNT, W. F., "Perspective for the Coming Decade," U.S. Senate Committee on Labor and Human Resources Hearings on *Workplace and Higher Education,* June 1979, U.S. Gov't. Printing Office, 1980.

BOK, DEREK, *Beyond the Ivory Tower,* Cambridge, Harvard University Press, 1982.

BOTKIN, JAMES, DAN DIMANCESCU AND RAY STATA, *Global Stakes,* Cambridge, Ballinger, 1982.

BOWEN, HOWARD R., *Investment in Learning,* San Francisco, Jossey-Bass, 1977.

BOWLES, SAMUEL, AND HERBERT GINTIS, *Schooling in Capitalist America,* New York, Basic Books, 1976.

BOYER, ERNEST L., AND FRED M. HECHINGER, *Higher Learning in the Nation's Service,* Washington, D.C., The Carnegie Foundation for the Advancement of Teaching, 1981.

BRANSCOMB, LEWIS M., AND PAUL C. GILMORE, "Education in Private Industry," *Daedalus,* p. 222 (Winter 1975).

Bricker's International Directory of University Executive Development Programs, Woodside, CA, Samuel C. Pond, 1981.

BROWNE, RICK, "Who Will Retrain Obsolete Managers," *Business Week,* April 25, 1983.

BRUBACHER, JOHN S., AND WILLIS RUDY, *Higher Education in Transition,* rev. ed., New York, Harper & Row, 1968.

BRUCE, JAMES D., WM. M. SILBERT, LOUIS D. SMULLIN AND ROBERT M. FANO, *Lifelong Cooperative Education,* Report of the Centennial Study Committee, Cambridge, M.I.T., 1982.

BULPITT, M., ed., *It's Your Business!,* Scottsdale, AZ, National League for Innovation, 1980.

BUREAU OF LABOR STATISTICS, USDL Document 82–276, U.S. Dept of Labor, Washington, D.C., Aug. 10, 1982.

CAHN, ROSANNE M., *The Pocket Chartroom,* New York, Goldman Sachs, 1983.

CAREY, MAX L., "Organizational Employment Growth Through 1990," *Monthly Labor Review,* 104, p. 42 (1981).

CARNEGIE COUNCIL ON HIGHER EDUCATION, *Three Thousand Futures,* San Francisco, Jossey-Bass, 1980.

CARNEVALE, ANTHONY P., "Cooperation for What?", in *Financing Higher Education: The Public Investment,* John C. Hoy and Melvin Bernstein, eds., Boston, Auburn Publishing House, 1982.

CARNEVALE, ANTHONY P., *Human Capital: A High Yield Corporate Investment,* Washington, D.C., Am. Soc. Training Dev., 1983.

CARNEVALE, ANTHONY P., AND HAROLD GOLDSTEIN, *Employee Training: Its Changing Role and an Analysis of New Data,* Washington, D.C., Am. Soc. Training Dev., 1983.

CHOATE, PAT, "American Workers at the Rubicon," *Commentary,* pp. 3–10 (Summer 1982).

CLECAK, PETER, "Views of Social Critics," in *Investment in Learning*, Howard R. Bowen, San Francisco, Jossey-Bass, 1977.

THE COOPERATIVE EDUCATION RECORD CENTER. *Undergraduate Programs of Cooperative Education in the U. S. and Canada*, Boston, Northeastern University, 1978.

CRAIG, ROBERT L., "Introduction to the Conference on the Nature and Extent of Employee Training and Development," *Proceedings of the ASTD National Issues Forum*, Washington, D.C., Am. Soc. Training Dev., 1983.

CRAIG, ROBERT L., AND CHRISTINE J. EVERS, "Employers and Educators: The Shadow Education System," in *New Directions for Experiential Learning: Business and Higher Education—Towards New Alliances*, Gerard G. Gold, ed., San Francisco, Jossey-Bass, 1981.

CROSS, K. PATRICIA, "New Frontiers for Higher Education: Business and Professions," in *Partnerships with Business and the Professions, 1981 Current Issues in Higher Education*, Washington, D.C., Am. Assoc. for Higher Ed., 1981.

DENISON, E. F., *The Sources of Economic Growth in the United States*, New York, Committee for Economic Development, 1962.

DENISON, E. F., *Accounting for United States Economic Growth, 1929–1969*, Washington, D.C., Brookings Institute, 1974.

Dictionary of Occupational Titles, U.S. Unemployment Service, 2 vols., 4th ed., Washington, Gov't Printing Office, 1977.

Digest of Education Statistics, 1981, Washington, National Center for Education Statistics, 1981.

Digest of Educational Statistics, 1964 edition, Washington, U.S. Department of Health, Education, and Welfare, 1964.

DORE, RONALD, *The Diploma Disease*, Berkeley, University of California Press, 1976.

DOUGLASS, GORDON K., "Economic Returns on Investment in Higher Education," in *Investment in Learning*, Howard R. Bowen, San Francisco, Jossey-Bass, 1977.

DRUCKER, PETER F., "What Can We Learn From Japanese Management," *Harvard Business Review*, p. 110 (Mar.–Apr., 1971).

DRUCKER, PETER F., ed., "Developing Management and Managers," in *Management*, New York, Harper & Row, 1973.

DRUCKER, PETER F., *The Age of Discontinuity*, paperback ed., New York, Harper & Row, 1978.

DRUCKER, PETER F., "As Education Heads into a 'Baby Bust,' Competition and Diversity Will Prevail," *Chronicle of Higher Education*, 22 (II), p. 56 (1981).

DUNLOP, JOHN T., *Human Resources: Toward Rational Policy Planning*, Report No. 669, New York, The Conference Board, 1975.

ELLUL, JACQUES, *The Technological Society*, New York, Knopf, 1964.

EMMERIJ, LOUIS, "Paid Educational Leave: A Proposal Based on the Dutch Case," in *Financing Recurrent Education*, Henry M. Levin and Hans G. Schütze, eds., Beverly Hills, Sage Publications, 1983.

ERNST, MARTIN L., "The Mechanization of Commerce," *Scientific American*, 247, No. 3, p. 132 (1982).

FEINBERG, WALTER, AND HENRY ROSEMONT, JR., eds., *Work, Technology and Education*, Urbana, University of Illinois Press, 1975.

FENWICK, DOROTHY C., ed., *Directory of Campus-Business Linkages*, New York, ACE/Macmillan, 1983.

FISHER, BERNICE M., *Industrial Education: American Ideals and Institutions*, Madison, University of Wisconsin Press, 1967.

FITCH, JOHN T., "A Consortium for Engineering Education," in *Communications Technology in Education and Training*, Silver Spring, Information Dynamics, Inc., 1982.

FRANKEL, MARTIN M., AND DEBRA E. GERALD, *Projections of Education Statistics to 1990–91*, Vol. I, Washington, D.C., National Center for Education Statistics, 1982.

FREEMAN, R. B., *The Over-Educated American*, New York, Academic Press, 1976.

FULLERTON, HOWARD N., JR., "The 1995 Labor Force: A First Look," in *Economic Projections to 1990*, Bureau of Labor Statistics Bulletin 2121, pp. 48–58, Washington, D.C., U.S. Dept. of Labor, Mar. 1982.

GIBBONS, J. F., W. R. KINCHELOE AND K. S. DOWN, "Tutored Videotape Instruction: A New Use of Electronic Media in Education," *Science*, 195, p. 1139 (1977).

GINZBERG, ELI, "The Mechanization of Work," *Scientific American*, 247, No. 3, pp. 66–75 (1982).

GINZBERG, ELI, AND GEORGE J. VOJTA, "The Service Sector of the U.S. Economy," *Scientific American*, 244, No. 3, pp. 48–55 (1981).

GIULIANO, VINCENT E., "The Mechanization of Office Work," *Scientific American*, 247, No. 3, p. 148 (1982).

GOLD, GERARD G., ed., *New Directions for Experiential Learning: Business and Higher Education—Toward New Alliances,* San Francisco, Jossey-Bass, 1981.

GOLD, GERARD G., AND IVAN CHARNER, "Employer-Paid Tuition Aid: Hidden Treasure," *Educational Record,* p. 45 (Spring 1983).

GOLDSTEIN, HAROLD, *Training and Education in Industry,* Washington, D.C., Nat'l. Inst. Work and Learning, 1980.

GOLDSTEIN, HAROLD, "Using Data on Employee Training from the Survey of Participation in Adult Education (C.P.S.)," *Proceedings of the ASTD National Issues Forum,* Washington, D.C., Am. Soc. Training Dev., 1983.

GORDON, MARGARET S., ed., *Higher Education and the Labor Market,* New York, McGraw-Hill, 1974.

GORDON, MORTON, "The Management of Continuing Education," in *Power and Conflict in Continuing Education,* Harold J. Alford, ed., Belmont, CA, Wadsworth, 1980.

GORLIN, HARRIET, *Personnel Practices I: Recruitment, Placement, Training, Communication,* Information Bulletin No. 89, New York, The Conference Board, 1981.

GUNN, THOMAS G., "The Mechanization of Design and Manufacturing," *Scientific American,* 247, No. 3, p. 114 (1982).

GURALNICK, S. A., "Deploying Educational Technology at an Independent, Urban Institution," in *Technology and Education,* Washington, D.C., Inst. Ed. Leadership, 1981.

HANDLIN, OSCAR, AND MARY F. HANDLIN, *The American College and American Culture—Socialization as a Function of Higher Education,* New York, McGraw-Hill, 1970.

HATALA, ROBERT J., "The Problem-Solving Model of Graduate Education," in *Expanding the Missions of Graduate and Professional Education,* Frederic Jacobs and Richard J. Allen, eds., San Francisco, Jossey-Bass, 1982.

HAWTHORNE, ELIZABETH M., PATRICIA A. LIBBY AND NANCY S. NASH, "The Emergence of Corporate Colleges," *Journal of Continuing Higher Education,* pp. 1–9 (Fall 1983), Vol. 31.

HAYES, ROBERT H., AND WILLIAM J. ABERNATHY, "Managing Our Way to Economic Decline," *Harvard Business Review,* pp. 67–77 (July–Aug., 1980).

HODGKINSON, H. L., "Guess Who's Coming to College," NIICU

Research Report, Washington, D.C., Nat'l. Inst. Indep. Colleges and Universities, 1982.

Hope Reports U.S. Training Business, Rochester, N.Y., Hope Reports, Inc., 1983.

HOULE, CYRIL, *Continuing Learning in the Professions,* San Francisco, Jossey-Bass, 1980.

HOWARD, ANN, AND DOUGLAS W. BRAY, "Career Motivation in Mid-Life Managers," Am. Psychol. Assoc. Annual Convention, Montreal (Sept. 1980).

HOY, JOHN C., "The Absence of National Policy," in *Financing Higher Education: The Public Investment,* John C. Hoy and Melvin H. Bernstein, Boston, Auburn Publishing House, 1982.

HOY, JOHN C., AND MELVIN H. BERNSTEIN, eds., *Business and Academia: Partners in New England's Economy,* Hanover, University Press of New England, 1981.

HOY, JOHN C., AND MELVIN H. BERNSTEIN, eds., *New England's Vital Resource: The Labor Force,* Washington, D.C., The American Council on Education, 1982a.

HOY, JOHN C., AND MELVIN H. BERNSTEIN, *Financing Higher Education: The Public Investment,* Boston, Auburn Publishing House, 1982b.

HUGHES, EVERETT C., "Higher Education and the Professions," in *Content and Context,* Carl Kaysen, ed., New York, McGraw-Hill, 1973.

IBM Annual Corporate Report for 1982, Armonk, N.Y., International Business Machines Corporation, 1983.

ILLICH, IVAN D., *Deschooling Society,* New York, Harper & Row, 1971.

JANGER, ALLEN R., *Matrix Organization of Complex Businesses,* Report No. 765, New York, The Conference Board, 1979.

JENCKS, CHRISTOPHER, AND DAVID RIESMAN, *The Academic Revolution,* Chicago, University of Chicago Press, 1968.

JOINER, WILLIAM, "Dilemmas in Experiential Learning Programs: Toward a Holistic Approach," in *Developing Experiential Learning Programs for Professional Education,* Eugene T. Byrne and Douglas E. Wolfe, eds., San Francisco, Jossey-Bass, 1980.

KAY EVELYN R., *Participation in Adult Education, 1981,* Washington, D.C., National Center for Education Statistics, 1982.

KAYSEN, CARL, ed., *Content and Context,* New York, McGraw-Hill, 1973.

KERR, CLARK, *The Uses of the University,* Cambridge, Harvard University Press, 1963.

KERR, CLARK, *The Uses of the University,* 3rd ed., Cambridge, Harvard University Press, 1982.

KIDDER, TRACY, *The Soul of a New Machine,* Boston, Little, Brown and Co., 1981.

KNOX, KATHLEEN, *Polaroid Corporation's Tuition Assistance Plan: A Case Study,* Washington, D.C., Nat'l. Mgmt. Inst. (now Nat'l. Inst. for Work and Learning), 1979.

KOST, ROBERT J., "Competition and Innovation in Continuing Education," in *Power and Conflict in Continuing Education,* Harold J. Alford, Belmont, CA, Wadsworth, 1980.

KUHLENKAMP, DETLEF, AND HANS GEORG SCHÜTZE, *Kosten u. Finanzierung der beruflichen u. nichtberuflichen Weiterbildung,* Frankfurt/M: Diesterweg, 1982.

LEONTIEFF, WASSILY W., "The Distribution of Work and Income," *Scientific American,* 247, No. 3, pp. 188–205 (1982).

LEVENTMAN, PAULA, *Skill/Knowledge Obsolescence: A Report on Re-Training Highly Skilled Technical Employees,* Bedford, MA, Digital Equipment Services, 1982.

LEVIN, HARRY M., AND RUSSELL W. RUMBERGER, "The Educational Implications of Higher Technology," Stanford, CA, Institute for Research on Educational Finance and Governance, 1983.

LEVIN, HARRY M., AND HANS G. SCHÜTZE, *Financing Adult Education,* Beverly Hills, CA, Sage Publications, 1983.

LINDBLOM, CHARLES E. AND DAVID K. COHEN, *Usable Knowledge: Social Science and Social Problem Solving,* New Haven, Yale University Press, 1979.

LINNELL, ROBERT H., "Professional Activities for Additional Income; Benefits and Problems," in *Dollars and Scholars,* Robert H. Linnell, ed., Los Angeles, University of Southern California Press, 1982.

LUSTERMAN, SEYMOUR, "Education in Industry," Report No. 719, New York, The Conference Board, 1977.

LUSTERMAN, SEYMOUR, "Managerial Competence: The Public Affairs Aspects," Report No. 805, New York, The Conference Board, 1981.

LUXENBERG, STAN, "Education at AT&T," *Change,* p. 26 (Dec.–Jan., 1978/1979).

Lynn, Kenneth S., Introduction, "The Professions," *Daedalus*, 92, No. 4 (Fall 1963).

Lynton, Ernest A., "Colleges, Universities and Corporate Training," in *New Directions for Experiential Learning: Business and Higher Education—Toward New Alliances*, Gerard G. Gold, ed., San Francisco, Jossey-Bass, 1981a.

Lynton, Ernest A., "A Role for Colleges in Corporate Training and Development," in *Current Issues in Higher Education*, Am. Assoc. Higher Ed., 1981b.

Lynton, Ernest A., "Improving Cooperation Between Colleges and Corporations," *Educational Record*, pp. 20–25 (Fall 1982a).

Lynton, Ernest A., "The Interdependence of Employment and Education," in *Massachusetts Higher Education in the Eighties: Manpower and the Economy*, Boston, The Alden Seminars, 1982b.

Lynton, Ernest A., "A Curriculum for Tomorrow's World," in *In Opposition to Core Curriculums*, James W. Hall and Barbara L. Kevles, eds., Westport, CT, Greenwood Press, 1982c.

Lynton, Ernest A., "The Role of Higher Education in Human Capital Formation and Maintenance," Boston, The Alden Seminars, 1983a.

Lynton, Ernest A., "Occupational Maintenance: Recurrent Education to Maintain Occupational Effectiveness," *CAEL News*, 7, No. 1 (Sept. 1983b), pp. 6–8, 19; No. 2 (Oct. 1983b), pp. 4–7, 15.

Lynton, Ernest A., "Reexamining the Role of the University," *Change*, 15, No. 7, 1983c.

Lynton, Ernest A., "Higher Education's Role in Fostering Employee Education," *Educational Records*, pp. 18–25 (Fall 1983d).

MacGregor, Douglas, *The Human Side of Enterprise*, New York, McGraw-Hill, 1960.

Machlup, Fritz, *The Production and Distribution of Knowledge in the U.S.*, Princeton, Princeton University Press, 1962.

Machlup, Fritz, *Education and Economic Growth*, Lincoln, NE, University of Nebraska Press, 1970.

Mahoney, James R., *Community College Centers for Contracted Programs*, Washington, Am. Assoc. Community and Junior Colleges, 1982.

Main, Jeremy, "Why Engineering Deans Worry a Lot," *Fortune*, pp. 84ff, Jan. 11, 1982.

Marovelli, Robert L., and John M. Karhnak, "The Mechanization of Mining," *Scientific American*, 247, p. 90 (1982).

MASNICK, GEORGE, "Demographic Influences on the Labor Force in New England," in *New England's Vital Resource: The Labor Force,* John C. Hoy and Melvin H. Bernstein, eds., Washington, D.C., The American Council on Ed., 1982.

McNULTY, NANCY, ed., *Management Development Programs: The World's Best,* Amsterdam, North Holland Co., 1980.

McPHERSON, MICHAEL S., "Higher Education: Investment or Expense?", in *Financing Higher Education: The Public Investment,* John C. Hoy and Melvin H. Bernstein, eds., Boston, Auburn Publishing House, 1982.

McPHERSON, MICHAEL S., "Value Conflicts In American Higher Education," *J. Higher Ed., 54,* pp. 243–278 (1983).

MEDOFF, JAMES L., "Labor Markets in Imbalance," mimeographed, Cambridge, Harvard University, November 1982.

MILLS, D. QUINN, "Human Resources in the '80's," *Harvard Business Review,* p. 154 (July–Apr., 1975),

MILLS, TED, "Human Resources—Why the New Concern?", *Harvard Business Review,* p. 120 (Mar.–Apr., 1975).

MORISON, ELTING E., *Men, Machines and Modern Times,* Cambridge, The MIT Press, 1966.

MOULTON, HARPER W., private communication, 1981.

The National Guide to Non-Collegiate Sponsored Education, Washington, American Council on Education, 1982.

NEUMANN, WILLIAM, "Educational Responses to the Concern for Proficiency," in *On Competence,* Gerald Grant et al., San Francisco, Jossey-Bass, 1979.

New York Times, "A Curriculum in Flux," C 21:1, Oct. 3, 1982.

1981–82 Fact Book for Academic Administrators, Washington, American Council on Education, 1981.

O'KEEFE, MICHAEL, *The Adult, Education and Public Policy,* Cambridge, Aspen Institute, 1977.

O'KEEFE, MICHAEL, "Statement by the General Rapporteur," *Policies for Higher Education in the 1980's,* Paris, OECD, 1983.

PARSONS, TALCOTT, AND GERALD M. PLATT, *The American University,* Cambridge, Harvard University Press, 1973.

PETERS, GIB, "A Consortium Approach to the Utilization of Television for the Delivery of Instruction to Business and Industry," in *Communications Technology in Education and Training,* Silver Springs, Information Dynamics, Inc., 1982.

PETERS, THOMAS J., AND ROBERT H. WATERMAN, JR., *In Search of Excellence,* New York, Harper & Row, 1982.

PETERSON, DAVID A., *Facilitating Education for Older Learners,* San Francisco, Jossey-Bass, 1983.

PETERSON, RICHARD E., "Issues in University Continuing Education in the United States," mimeographed, Paris, OECD 1983.

PETERSON, RICHARD E., et al., *Adult Education and Training in Industrialized Countries,* New York, Praeger, 1982.

PHILLIPS, LOUIS E., "Trends in State Relicensure," in *Power and Conflict in Continuing Education,* Vol. II, Milton R. Stern, ed., Belmont, CA, Wadsworth, 1983.

PORAT, MARC U., *The Information Economy,* 9 vols., Washington, D.C., U. S. Gov't. Printing Office, 1977.

RASMUSSEN, WAYNE D., "The Mechanization of Agriculture," *Scientific American,* 247, No. 3, p. 76 (1982).

RAWLINGS, V. LANE, AND LLOYD ULMAN, "The Utilization of College-Trained Manpower in the United States," in *Higher Education and the Labor Market,* Margaret S. Gordon, ed., New York, McGraw-Hill, 1974.

Recruiting Trends, "Tuition-Aid Helps Fulfill Affirmative Action Programs," Sept. 1979.

Regents Guide, 1980: A Guide to Educational Programs in Non-Collegiate Organizations, Albany, University of the State of New York, 1980.

REICH, ROBERT B., *The Next American Frontier,* New York, Times Books, 1983. A summary appeared in *Atlantic Monthly,* Mar. and Apr. 1983.

ROSENBERG, RONALD, "Keeping Track of the 'Engineer Shortage,'" *The Boston Globe,* p. 40, Dec. 15, 1981.

ROSOW, LESLIE A., *Kimberley-Clark Corporation's Educational Opportunities Plan: A Case Study,* Washington, D.C., Nat'l. Manpower Inst. (now Nat'l. Inst. for Work and Learning), 1979.

RUMBERGER, RUSSELL W., "The Changing Skill Requirements of Jobs in the U.S. Economy," *Ind. Labor Rel. Rev.* 84, p. 578 (1981).

RUMBERGER, RUSSELL W., *The Job Market for College Graduates,* mimeographed, Stanford University, December 1982.

SCHEIN, EDGAR H., WITH DIANE W. KOMMERS, *Professional Education,* New York, McGraw-Hill, 1972.

SCHEIN, EDGAR H., "Increasing Organizational Effectiveness Through

Better Human Resource Planning and Development," *Sloan Mgmt. Rev.*, 19, p. 1 (1977).

SCHILLINGER, A. GEORGE, HAROLD G. KAUFMAN AND ANTHONY J. WILNER, *New Directions in Continuing Education: Changing Roles of Universities, Industry, and Government*, St. Louis, MO, Industrial Research Institute/Research Corporation, 1978. .

SCHÖN, DONALD A., *The Reflective Practitioner: How Professionals Think in Action*, New York, Basic Books, 1983a.

SCHÖN, DONALD A., unpublished manuscript, 1983b.

SCHULTZ, T. W., "Education and Economic Growth," in *Social Forces Influencing American Education:* Chicago, Nat'l. Society for the Study of Education, 1961.

SCHULTZ, T. W., *The Economic Value of Education*, New York, Columbia University Press, 1963.

SCOTT, JOAN WALLACK, "The Mechanization of Woman's Work," *Scientific American*, 247, No. 3, p. 166 (1982).

SHAEFFER, RUTH G., *Staffing Systems, Managerial and Professional Jobs*, Report No. 558, New York, The Conference Board, 1972.

SHAEFFER, RUTH G., AND ALLEN R. JANGER, *Who Is Top Management?*, Report No. 821, New York, The Conference Board, 1982.

SHORE, JANE, *The Education Fund of District Council 37: A Case Study*, Washington, D.C., Nat'l. Manpower Inst. (now Nat'l. Inst. for Work and Learning), 1979.

SIMMONS, JOHN, AND WILLIAM MARES, *Working Together*, New York, Knopf, 1983.

SKROVAN, DANIEL J., ed., *Quality of Work Life: Perspectives for Business and the Public Sector*, Washington, D.C., American Society for Training and Development, 1983.

SMELSER, NEIL J., "Growth, Structural Change, and Conflict in California Public Higher Education, 1950–1970," in *Public Higher Education in California*, Neil J. Smelser and Gabriel Almond, eds., Berkeley, Univ. of California Press, 1974.

STARCEVICH, MATT M., AND J. ARNOLD SYKE, "Internal Advanced Management Program for Executive Development," *Human Resource Planning* 3, p. 97 (1980).

STERN, MILTON R., "Universities in Continuing Education," in *Power and Conflict in Continuing Education*, Harold J. Alford, Belmont, CA, Wadsworth, 1980.

TAYLOR, F. W., *Scientific Management and Job Analysis*, New York, Harper & Row, 1947 (originally published in 1911).

TICHY, NOEL, CHARLES J. FOMBRUN AND MARY ANNE DEVANNA, "Strategic Human Resource Management," *Sloan Mgmt. Rev.* 8, p. 47 (1982).

TIERNEY, MICHAEL, "Public Policy Issues and the Current Population Survey," *Proceedings of the ASTD National Issues Forum*, Washington, D.C., Am. Soc. Training Dev., 1983.

VEBLEN, THORSTEN, *The Higher Learning in America*, New York, Kelly, 1918.

VEYSEY, LAURENCE R., *The Emergence of the American University*, Chicago, University of Chicago Press, 1965.

WALKER, JAMES W., "Linking Human Resource Planning and Strategic Planning," *Human Resource Planning* 1, p. 101 (1978).

WEINSTEIN, LAURENCE M., "Employers in the Private Sector," in *The Costs and Financing of Adult Education*, Richard Anderson, ed., New York, Lexington Books, 1982.

WHITEHEAD, ALFRED NORTH, *The Aims of Education*, New York, Macmillan Co., 1929.

WIRTZ, WILLARD, *Tuition-Air Revisited: Tapping the Untapped Resource*, Washington, D.C., Nat'l. Manpower Inst. (now Nat'l. Inst. for Work and Learning), 1979.

WYKSTRA, RONALD A., *Education and the Economics of Human Capital*, New York, The Free Press, 1971.

YARRINGTON, ROGER, "Partnerships for Education and Employment," *Catalyst* 8, pp. 5–9 (1977).

YARRINGTON, ROGER, ed., "Employee Training for Productivity," Washington, D.C., Am. Assoc. Community and Jr. Colleges, 1980.

YOUNG, ANNE MCDOUGALL, "Trends in Educational Attainment Among Workers in the 1970's," in *Special Labor Force Report 240*, U.S. Dept. of Labor, Bureau of Labor Statistics (Jan. 1981).

YOUNG, ANNE MCDOUGALL, "Recent Trends in Higher Education and Labor Force Activity," *Monthly Labor Review*, pp. 39–41 (Feb. 1983).

ZEMKE, R., "U.S. Training Census and Trends Report, 1982–83," Minneapolis, Lakewood Publications, 1983. A condensation of the report has been published in *Training*, p. 22ff (Oct. 1983).

Name and Title Index

This index includes the names of individuals, organizations, and publications.

Subject Index